Unclutter
Your
Home

7 Simple Steps
700 Tips & Ideas

Donna Smallin

**STOREY
BOOKS**

The mission of Storey Publishing is to serve our customers by publishing practical information that encourages personal independence in harmony with the environment.

Edited by Gwen Steege and Janet Lape
Cover design by Meredith Maker
Cover and interior illustrations by Carleen Powell
Text design and production by Susan Bernier
Indexed by Barbara Hagerty

Printed in the United States by R.R. Donnelley
10 9 8

Library of Congress Cataloging-in-Publication Data

Smallin, Donna, 1960-
       Unclutter your home : 7 simple steps, 700 tips & ideas /
Donna Smallin.
              p. cm.
       Includes index.
       ISBN 1-58017-108-7 (pbk. : alk. paper)
       1. Storage in the home. 2. House cleaning. I. Title.
TX309 .S63   1999
648—dc21   98-47041
                                                        CIP

Contents

Dedication

For my husband, Terry, and all the precious moments we share in love and laughter, peace and harmony.

Acknowledgments

With heartfelt gratitude to my friends, colleagues, and family members: Thank you for your wonderful suggestions and true confessions. You gave my brain the jump start it needed to get this book rolling.

To the professional organizers who so readily shared their knowledge and expertise, I wish you continued success and happiness. Many thanks to:

Gloria Ritter, President of PaperMatters & more, inc., in Washington, D.C., and 1997–99 President of the National Association of Professional Organizers;

Judith Kolberg, Director of the National Study Group on Chronic Disorganization and President of FileHeads Professional Organizers in Avondale Estates, Georgia;

Sandra Felton, author of numerous books for "messies" and founder of Messies Anonymous;

Barbara Hemphill, author of *Kiplinger's Taming the Paper Tiger* and *Kiplinger's Taming the Office Tiger,* and President of Hemphill & Associates in Raleigh, North Carolina;

Debbie Williams, President of Let's Get It Together, a Houston, Texas–based, on-line organizing service;

Jann Jasper, a New York City–based productivity consultant and author of *Strategic Time Management* (1999);

Helen Volk, President of Beyond Clutter in Albany, New York; and

Anne Halabuda, President of International Organizing in Voorheesville, New York.

thank you!

For the opportunity to write this book, I thank my lucky stars and my editors and friends at Storey Books for having faith in me.

Introduction

I got into the habit of saving stuff, because . . . well, because it was *my* stuff. As a kid, I never had much in the way of material possessions. So I treasured each new acquisition, whether it was something I bought or something that was given to me. And I saved everything.

Try as I might, I just couldn't bring myself to throw away anything, especially something that was still perfectly good, like the beautiful white linen material I once bought to make a dress. I got as far as cutting out the pattern, but then set it aside for one reason or another. I had every intention of finishing that dress — someday. Ten years and three moves later, I finally threw out the whole thing. And you know what? It was a relief to be rid of it.

What I have discovered is that it takes a certain amount of courage to let go of the bits and pieces of our lives that we no longer need. But letting go can set you free in body, mind, and spirit.

Every time I looked at that unfinished dress, it was a reminder of one more thing I needed to do. Even after I put it away in a closet, the feeling of unfinished business would wash over me whenever I happened to catch a glimpse of that white linen fabric.

You might get that same feeling when you look at the piles of stuff on your dining-room table or the mounds of clothes in your bedroom or the helter-skelter state of your basement or garage.

Material possessions demand our attention. They need to be put away, cleaned, maintained, and repaired. And the more possessions we have, the more time we need to spend caring for them. The feeling that you need to do something with your possessions can really sap your energy, leaving you feeling physically tired and emotionally drained.

Life is so much simpler when you have only what you need. I'm not suggesting that you get rid of everything you own and take a vow of poverty. But if you can bring yourself to let go of the things you no longer love or use, you will gain more time and energy for living, loving, and celebrating life.

Imagine for a moment what it must be like to have no clutter in your home. Nothing to step over or push aside. No mess. No chaos. Just beautiful, peaceful, serene order all around you.

The difference between clutter and order, chaos and peace is quite simply a choice. A choice that only you can make.

A 19th-century philosopher by the name of Jeremy Bentham proposed that people make either/or decisions by weighing the pain against the pleasure. When you weigh the pain of letting go against the pleasure of living a simpler, more beautiful life, the choice becomes clear. All you need to do then is make a commitment and the rest will take care of itself.

Once your home is ordered, you will feel more satisfied with yourself and at peace with the world. You'll have more time to nurture yourself and the people you share your life with. Time to relax. Time to express yourself through the arts or to pursue a lifelong dream.

> *Time is a very precious gift — so precious that it is only given to us moment by moment.*
>
> — Amelia Barr

Escape the Chaos

By following the seven simple steps outlined in this book, you can escape the chaos of your cluttered existence and perhaps even begin to accomplish more of what matters most to you.

Following is an overview of the seven steps to unclutter your home:

- **Step 1: Assess your situation.** It's helpful to understand how and why clutter happens and to recognize how it's affecting the quality of your life.
- **Step 2: Plan for success.** If you establish the proper attitude, motivation, and environment for changing old habits, you can create lasting change.

- **Step 3: Lighten your load.** Free up space and time by letting go of things you don't love or need or use anymore.
- **Step 4: Contain yourself.** Find a place for everything so you can always put everything in its place.
- **Step 5: Revamp clutter zones.** Minimize clutter by organizing your home and possessions to fit your lifestyle.
- **Step 6: Simplify with systems.** Organize and simplify your life with systems for handling routine chores and tasks.
- **Step 7: Ban clutter forever.** Learn how to maintain your new, clutter-free lifestyle.

This book is full of simple, practical, proven tips for uncluttering your home. Some may be reminders of things you forgot; others may confirm that you've got the right idea. Even exceptionally organized people are sure to find a few gems, including ideas for high-tech uncluttering — ways you can use your computer to sell or

---

If solid happiness we prize,
Within our breast this jewel lies
And they are fools who roam.
The world has nothing to bestow;
From our own selves our joys must
flow,
And that dear hut, our home.

— Nathaniel Cotton

---

barter unwanted items, find organizing services and products, minimize paper mess, and more.

Clutter won't disappear overnight, but you can start uncluttering now and see progress almost immediately. It may take a little time. After all, your house didn't get cluttered overnight. Uncluttering for good is a lot like losing weight and keeping it off. You spent months and years putting on the pounds and you have to allow time to lose it. We all know that lose-weight-quick schemes are just a quick fix. What you need is a long-term solution. The same is true for getting rid of clutter.

Start today and keep at it. Be patient. Your reward will be well worth the wait.

Assess Your Situation

In this chapter . . .

- *What's Your Clutter Quotient?*
- *Why Clutter Happens*
- *The Cost of Clutter*
- *The Rewards of Uncluttering*

What is clutter? How did I end up with so much of it? Is it really possible for me to eliminate clutter?

Clutter is anything for which you have no use or need — everything from outgrown clothes to expired coupons. It's stuff you don't want anymore — things you bought too soon or held on to for too long. Uncluttering is the act of restoring balance to your life by eliminating these unimportant things — and doing it will free up time, energy, and space for the things that really matter.

You *can* get rid of clutter. No matter how much stuff you own, or how small your home, or how little time you have to spare, you can transform chaos into order by following the seven simple steps outlined in this book.

What's Your Clutter Quotient?

The first step is to assess your situation. Try this simple exercise. Walk out the front door, close it behind you, and turn around. (Come on, do it!)

Pretend you are a neighbor or friend who has never been to your house. Invite yourself in! Now, look around as if you are seeing your home for the first time. What's your first impression? On a scale of 1 to 10, with 10 being the most favorable impression, how would you rate your first impression of your home? How far off is your impression from the impression you would like to make?

In assessing your situation, it helps to think of your home as a reflection of yourself — your interests, beliefs, and passions. What does your home tell others about you? Where there's clutter, there's confusion — not just in your home, but in your life.

For some people, clutter is a temporary state. You let it build for one reason or another — lack of time, too many commitments — but at some point, you just look around and say, "Yuck!" and immediately start uncluttering.

For others, clutter has become a way of life. You look back and can't remember a time when you weren't buried under piles of papers and books, heaps of clothing, overflowing closets and drawers. Just looking at it all makes you feel frustrated, overwhelmed, tired.

FINDING YOUR CLUTTER QUOTIENT

Choose a number (1–4) that best describes your response to each of the following statements.

1 = Never or almost never   3 = Usually
2 = Sometimes   4 = All the time

____ When I have free time, I like to shop.

____ I keep bills, bank statements, and other mail in piles, until I have time to file.

____ I have more than 10 plastic shopping bags in my house.

____ I save magazines with interesting articles/recipes.

____ When I look around, I get tired just thinking about what it will take to unclutter my home.

____ I have two or more craft projects going at any one time.

____ My house may look messy to some people, but I know where to find everything.

____ If someone stops by unexpectedly, I try to avoid letting them in.

____ I leave things out so I know where they are or as a reminder to myself.

What's your situation? Are you just temporarily disorganized or does clutter control your life?

Fortunately, even the most chronically disorganized people can change their behavior with the right motivation and a little self-discipline. It requires some effort, but it is simple once you learn to take control of clutter.

___ Time keeps me from getting or being organized.

___ When it comes to clutter, I think, "Why bother?" It will just get cluttered again.

___ I can't bear to part with things and I consider myself a pack rat.

___ The stress level in our house is directly related to the clutter level.

___ TOTAL

Rating Your Answers

Add up your score. A score of 44–52 is indicative of a clutter problem that's been building for some time. You are in need of some serious clutter-busting! If you scored 35–43, your clutter problem is likely growing worse with each passing year and will continue to do so unless you do something about it. If your score totaled 26–34, you have the potential to develop a clutter problem, but you also have the power to change a few old habits. If you scored 17–25, you may be temporarily disorganized. Following the seven simple steps outlined in this book, it won't take long to get your home in order. If you scored less than 17, congratulations on controlling clutter, rather than letting it control you.

Why Clutter Happens

Like it or not, clutter happens. If you want to get rid of clutter, it helps to understand how and why clutter happens and, more importantly, why it happens to nice people like you.

The root of clutter can be traced to a number of sources. One reason we have so much of it is because our lives have become increasingly complex over the past 20 to 30 years. More moms work outside their homes and growing numbers of men and women are working two jobs.

PERCENTAGE OF MARRIED WOMEN WORKING OUTSIDE THE HOME

	AGE 25–34	35–44	45–64
1970	38.8%	46.8%	44.0%
1996	71.7%	75.8%	63.7%

From *The Statistical Abstract of the United States 1997*, U.S. Department of Commerce, Bureau of the Census

Remember when Sunday used to be a day of rest? You spent the whole day at home with your family or you all hopped into the station wagon and headed off to visit Grandma and Grandpa.

Now we're all rushing off in different directions every day of the week. We can't keep up with each other, let alone the clutter. And when we stop, we're too darn tired to deal with it.

Tomorrow, we say. Or the next day. Or someday, for sure.

You are either a part of the solution or a part of the problem.

— Eldridge Cleaver

Add to our lack of time the fact that we've acquired a hefty volume of possessions which has prompted us to move into a larger house. The size of the average American home has nearly doubled over the last 50 years and the amount of possessions in our homes has increased along with it.

Many of us go shopping with nothing particular in mind. But we always come home with something. The more we earn, the more we spend — and the more we own. We just keep bringing stuff into our already cluttered homes, and creating more stress by digging ourselves deeper in debt. According to the December 1997 Consumer Federation of America report, credit-card balances climbed 6 percent to approximately $529 billion nationally in 1997.

So now we've got all of this stuff, and some of it has been with us for so long we've become quite attached to it. Oh, once in a while we throw out something or give it away, but mostly we hold on to our stuff because we can't bear to let it go — even things we may not need or use anymore.

Our emotional attachment to our stuff accounts for a great deal of clutter. How could you possibly part with the dress you were wearing when your husband proposed to you? Or your firstborn child's kindergarten artwork? Or some other belonging that invokes happy memories of years past?

Other times you keep belongings because you think you might need them in the future. You might, for example, be in the habit of saving travel brochures and maps, magazines, shopping bags, rubber bands, or twist ties.

And sometimes you hang on to your stuff because of the past *and* the future. Women, in particular, tend to keep clothing that doesn't fit anymore (past). If you give it away, it's like throwing away your hope (future) that someday you'll fit into it again!

In many cases, clutter develops from an instinct for self-preservation and feelings of insecurity. We surround ourselves with the familiarity of our stuff, blocking ourselves off from the people and possibilities that have the potential to create true happiness and security in our lives.

Another reason clutter collects is indecisiveness or deferred decision making. This is especially true of perfectionists. Think about it: If you're a perfectionist, you want to do everything just right — or not at all. So if you haven't got the time to organize your filing cabinet, you put it off and keep putting it off. Judith Kolberg, Director of the National Study Group on Chronic Disorganization, says, "Often, our best intentions are left in stacks."

The main reason people can't unclutter their homes is that they need help getting started. If that's why you bought this book, good for you for recognizing that you might need a little help!

TOP 10 REASONS WHY CLUTTER COLLECTS

1. You think you'll need it someday.
2. It has sentimental value.
3. You've got a big house.
4. You've got a small house.
5. You are chronically disorganized.
6. You leave stuff out because you're afraid you'll never find it again.
7. You feel guilty about throwing away things.
8. You feel like you never have time to get organized.
9. You were brought up by pack rats.
10. You're stuck on the "work, shop, spend" treadmill.

The Cost of Clutter

Clutter takes the joy out of living. It's frustrating when you can't find what you're looking for and maddening when things get ruined because they weren't properly stored. These negative feelings create negative energy in your home — and in your life. Change your surroundings and you can change your life, according to proponents of *feng shui,* the Taoist art and science of living in harmony with the environment.

Feng shui (pronounced fung shway) is based on the belief that your home is alive with energy. Through the doors and windows, it breathes in and out and its breath flows throughout the house, down the hallways and around every room. When its breath flows freely, you will enjoy sensations of ease and comfort. If clutter obstructs its flow, the elements in your body become unbalanced, and your health and affairs suffer.

At the very least, clutter wastes time that you can never get back. And disorganization can really take its toll on your life — physically, emotionally, socially, financially, and spiritually. Think about how it impacts you:

- **The physical cost.** How often are you late for an appointment or for work because you can't find your keys or something you need to bring with you? Do you often misplace notes, bills, or important documents? Disorganization creates unnecessary stress, and too much stress over a prolonged period can lead to serious health problems. Just think of the energy you waste each day, searching for things. No wonder you always feel tired! Being surrounded by piles of magazines and newspapers and other clutter, not to mention wading through it, is fatiguing in itself. It's also much more time-consuming to have to clean around clutter.

- **The emotional cost.** If you have too much clutter, it's a constant struggle to get through your day. There's always something standing in the way between you and your goals. Even small amounts of disorganization can make you feel out of control and create feelings of dissatisfaction with yourself and your life. The tendency to hold on to things is an attempt to fill a void in your life that can never be filled with things. But things just get in the way. Make a conscious choice to get rid of them and make room for the things that can fulfill and sustain your life.

- **The social cost.** Have you ever missed a lunch date or realized that you forgot a friend's birthday because the paper you wrote on to remind yourself got mixed in with your bills or other mail? When is the last time you invited anyone to your home? Clutter sometimes causes people to isolate themselves from friends and family. Uncluttering will free you to invite others into your home and your heart.

- **The financial cost.** How often do you buy something to replace something that was lost, only to find the original item at a later date? How often do you buy on impulse only to discover that you really don't like or need what you bought? If you "shop 'til you drop," clutter is the price you pay. And if you're paying on credit, you'll be paying for your purchases long after their usefulness has expired.

- **The spiritual cost.** Material possessions are yet another distraction from getting in touch with ourselves and our higher power. How can you be at peace when you always feel that something is lost or late? When you get rid of the material clutter in your life, you set the stage for peace and harmony in your home, relationships, and life. You can focus on what's really important to you.

The Rewards of Uncluttering

You might feel that you never have time to unclutter, but the reality is that uncluttering your home will simplify your life and give you more time.

By letting go of things you don't love or need or use — and organizing what's left — you will be able to find things more quickly and easily. And you will be creating a whole new way of life that is simpler and less stressful.

- **Trade chaos for serenity.** Imagine coming home to a peaceful, orderly environment of your own making — a place where you can escape the chaotic world around you.
- **Add hours to your day and days to your month.** A by-product of organization is efficiency. The more efficient you become, the more time you save, which means you gain time to spend with the people you love and on what you long to do.
- **Create positive change in other areas of your life.** Letting go of material possessions can be a mechanism for letting go of excess in other areas of your life. If you have more time to plan meals and get out for a walk, you may find it easier to lose weight. If you think twice before buying things, you may find yourself in a better financial position with less debt and more savings.

- **Set the stage for real happiness and success.** By simplifying your life and focusing on what's really important to you, you are more likely to achieve your definition of success.

There's no time like the present to begin experiencing the rewards of uncluttering. You've assessed your situation. Now it's time to plan for success.

Anything less than a conscious commitment to the important is an unconscious commitment to the unimportant.

— Stephen R. Covey, Ph.D.
First Things First

Plan for Success

In this chapter . . .

- *Establish Your Motivation*
- *Choose to Change Your Ways*
- *Envision Order*
- *Acknowledge Your Accomplishments*
- *Getting Organized*
- *Getting Help*

If you don't know where you are going, how will you know when you get there? Planning for success requires three decisions. You need to decide (1) what you want, (2) when you want it, and (3) what you will do to achieve it.

*Planning is bringing the future
into the present so that you can do
something about it now.*

— Alan Lakein

To create your plan for success, write down your answers to the following questions. Ask yourself:

- Why do I want to unclutter my home?
- What do I hope to accomplish?
- What am I willing to do?
- Why am I willing to do this now?
- How will I know when I am done?
- When do I want to be done?

It's important to set a realistic time frame for completing your goal. Then give yourself three to four weeks of daily uncluttering before evaluating your progress. If, after you get started, you realize that uncluttering your home may take longer than you thought, simply adjust your time frame for completion. And if you finish ahead of schedule, reward yourself by inviting friends or family to help you enjoy the beautiful home you've created!

Establish Your Motivation

If you want to unclutter your home once and for all, take some time to figure out what's important to you. In the process of determining what you value, you may learn something about yourself.

Try the following exercises. To get the maximum benefit from these exercises, you may want to jot down your thoughts.

If you had 20 minutes to evacuate your home and could only take what you could fit in your car, what would you take? What if you could only take what you could carry?

Once you realize that most things can be replaced, it's easier to lighten your load (see step 3).

~

Of what accomplishments are you most proud? What sacrifices, if any, did you make to achieve your successes?

Your past accomplishments are proof that you can do anything you put your mind to doing. Believe in yourself.

~

If you were to die tomorrow, what might people say about you at your funeral? Try to be as objective as you can. What would your children say about you? Your siblings? Your friends? Your colleagues? What would you like to have been remembered for? What personal qualities? What accomplishments or contributions?

If you want to be remembered as someone who was always giving to others, begin now by giving away the things you own that are just taking up space in your home. When you give to those who are more needy than you, you give yourself the gift of giving.

What do you dislike about clutter? In what ways do clutter and disorganization negatively affect your life? Why is it important for you to unclutter your home? What do you hope to gain?

The confusion in your home can spill over into the rest of your life, causing problems in your family or relationships. You may want to simplify your life just to prove to others that you can get organized and stay organized if you want to. Or maybe you need to make room in your life for something very important — perhaps a relationship. It doesn't matter what your reason is, but you need a reason that makes sense to you. Make that your motivation.

Make a list of your five favorite activities. Now write next to each one the date you last did these things.

Are you enjoying your favorite activities as often as you would like? Now here's a powerful motivation to simplify and organize your home — more time for you to learn and grow, relax and play! Do it for you.

Choose to Change Your Ways

Whether you realize it or not, you made a choice to let clutter build in your home. Actually, you probably made a lot of little choices over a long period of time. You chose to pile rather than file. Or you chose to keep buying things without getting rid of anything. Or you chose (consciously or subconsciously) to postpone making decisions about where to store things. Now you are living with the consequences of those choices and you don't like it.

So what can you do? It's simple. Make some new choices. Choose to start uncluttering your home and your life. Choose to start today and to keep at it until you are completely satisfied.

That's the wonderful thing about choice. No matter what choices you've made in the past, you can always make new choices. Start now by choosing to change the habits that got you where you are today.

$\sim$

Did you know that it takes 21 consecutive days to establish a new habit? That means you have to make a conscious effort every day *not* to do the same old thing.

$\sim$

If you want a more organized home, it helps to think like an organized person. Better yet, start telling yourself that you *are* an organized person because you have made a choice to be more organized. If you believe that you are organized, you will become organized.

$\sim$

Resolve not to create any more clutter in your home. Before you put something down, ask yourself, "Is this where it belongs?"

Do not postpone until tomorrow what should be done today. Delaying usually results in more work later, not to mention more time, more stress, and sometimes even more money.

Think first, act later. Next time you start to throw your coat over the back of a chair, stop! Don't do it. Hang it up. This will feel like work at first, but if you stick to it, eventually you will head straight for the closet when you come in. Once you develop this habit, it will become second nature and will no longer feel like work. In fact, it will feel like more work to hang up your coat twice. It *is* more work!

Never enter or leave a room without improving its appearance. Make every trip count. When you go to the basement, attic, garage, and up or down stairs, take something with you to put away.

To change your life, follow the advice of Dr. William James, the founder of modern psychology:

- Start immediately.
- Do it flamboyantly.
- Make no exceptions.

Purposely slow down. Take time out to do nothing. Just close your eyes, follow each breath with your mind, and listen to your thoughts.

Focus on doing one thing at a time. If you are organizing your closet, concentrate on doing it with excellence. If you're talking on the telephone with a friend, give this friend your undivided attention. If you're watching a television show or movie, enjoy it without doing anything else. Don't kid yourself into believing that it's more efficient to do two things at once. There's a difference between efficiency and effectiveness.

Envision Order

Uncluttering is not so much a matter of time management as it is mind management. As long as you believe that you have no control over clutter,

REGAIN CONTROL

In her book, *Sacred Space*, Denise Linn proposes that "our homes are symbolic representations of ourselves" and offers advice for changing your life by changing the energy in your home. Linn makes this comment about getting organized: "If your life feels full of confusion, the simple task of cleaning out your dresser drawers and making them spectacularly neat will spill over into the rest of your life. The sense of control and order that you gain from organizing your drawers can give you a sense of power and order in your life, and you may suddenly be able to solve problems which you felt completely befuddled about previously."

clutter will control you. But you can just as easily use your mind to put an end to clutter. If you can envision order, you can create it. It might help to find a picture of a home that's beautiful to you and put it somewhere where you can see it every day.

If previous attempts at uncluttering failed because of lack of motivation, or if the thought of getting organized makes you feel anxious or overwhelmed, try using some visualization techniques.

Take a good look around you. Now close your eyes and visualize what the room might look like without clutter. Give yourself some time. Can you can see it in your mind's eye?

Upon awakening each day or whenever you have a few moments to yourself, visualize your beautiful home. Visualization can be a powerful motivational tool. Someday, in the not-too-distant future, you will be able to look at your beautiful home and say, "It's just as I pictured it!"

Affirmations are another way to help you reach your goal of an uncluttered home. An affirmation is a positive statement with personal meaning that you repeat often. Here's an example of an affirmation you might use as you proceed toward your goal of uncluttering your home: "I am doing this out of love and respect for myself and my family."

Whatever you can do or dream you can, begin it. Boldness has beauty, power and magic in it.

— Johann von Goethe

Acknowledge Your Accomplishments

As with any change in lifestyle, self-discipline plays an important role. In her book *Inner Simplicity,* Elaine St. James introduces a game you can play to help develop self-discipline through a simple reward system. She recommends that you get a calendar and a box of gold stars (the kind you used to get in grade school). Each night, look back over your day. If you did one thing to reduce clutter in your home, place a gold star on that date in your calendar. Your goal is to give yourself a gold star every day of the month. If you don't get a gold star one day, don't worry about it. Just keep playing the game. Once you've got stars on every single day of the month, you've established a pattern of self-discipline you can apply to any area of your life.

As you work your way through a room, keep a list of things you need to do. Cross things off your list as you do them. It reminds you of what you have accomplished. At the end of one month, look at your list and you'll see you have made progress.

Don't look for "strokes" from other folks. Give yourself a stroke every day for committing your time and energy to uncluttering and simplifying your life.

Work quietly toward your goal and see how long it takes for others to notice what's going on around them.

⁓

Plan a celebration for the day you finish uncluttering that last room.

⁓

Reward yourself at steps along the way. Go out to lunch with a friend or go see a movie. Just don't go shopping for more stuff.

⁓

As you work on uncluttering your home, remember that you are learning new habits. If you slip up, don't give up.

Getting Organized

If you've taken a lot of heat throughout your life for being disorganized, cut yourself some slack. There are far worse things in life than being disorganized. It doesn't make you a bad person. It's not even a bad thing in and of itself. It's just that being disorganized makes even the simplest of things so much more difficult and stressful. And all that unpleasantness can get in the way of realizing your full potential.

Believe it or not, organized people weren't necessarily born organized. It's something they learned. They may have learned it from their parents. Or they may have learned it out of necessity.

(Try moving from a twelve-room house to a six-room apartment.) You can learn how to be organized just like you can learn anything you want to learn — by watching people who do it well or through trial and error. Discipline is required, because organization is a process. It's not something you can do just once and be done. It takes a certain amount of self-discipline to stay organized.

Keep in mind that there's a difference between being organized and being neat. Neatness is having everything nice and tidy. It's a by-product of organization. Being organized is being able to find what you need when you need it.

Try not to make any resolutions about getting organized. Jann Jasper, a NYC-based productivity consultant, believes that resolutions are usually based on what you think you should do and not on what you value. That's what makes it so difficult to follow through on a resolution. She advises a more effective strategy:

- Think in terms of goals, not resolutions.
- Figure out what's stopping you; address that first.
- Set motivating but realistic goals. Don't set yourself up for failure.

Goals begin behaviors.
Consequences maintain them.

— Kenneth Blanchard and Spencer Johnson,
The One-Minute Manager

SPACE, TIME, AND POSSESSIONS

Gloria Ritter, professional organizer and President of PaperMatters and more, inc., in Washington, D.C., says that most people will cite lack of time as the reason they are disorganized, when in reality, it is more often a lack of organizational skills. She recommends the STP Method for getting organized and says, "If you use it, it will increase your performance." The STP Method involves three elements:

- **Space.** Think about how you use your space. Be creative. An old pine dresser that's not being used might be perfect for storing candles, napkins, or paper plates in your dining room.
- **Time.** Learn how to manage your time. Try scheduling your free time first. Then schedule focused time for productive work. Don't waste a minute of that time. All the time in between is buffer time you can use for doing routine chores.
- **Possessions.** Inventory what you own. Because space and time are limited resources, you need to set limits on your possessions. As you decide what to keep — and before bringing anything new into your home — think about what impact it will have on your life in terms of space and time.

Ritter believes that the whole point of organization is to live life. The more organized you become, the more time you have to pursue your dreams.

Getting Help

If you can't do your own plumbing, you call a professional. If you're having difficulty uncluttering your home, call a professional organizer. A professional organizer can provide you with ideas, information, structure, solutions, and systems to help you regain control over your time and space. There are more than 800 professional organizers across the United States and beyond. To find a professional organizer near you, look in the yellow pages under "Organizing Services" or call the National Association of Professional Organizers' referral line at (512) 206-0151.

There's also an organization called Messies Anonymous, which was founded in 1981 as an educational and motivational aid for chronically disorganized individuals. In addition to offering a quarterly newsletter, books, and other materials, Messies Anonymous sponsors 12-step support groups in which participants set goals, discuss problems, and celebrate victories. For more information, contact Messies Anonymous, 5025 SW 114th Avenue, Miami, FL 33165; (800) MESS-AWAY; http://www.messies.com; E-mail: info@messies.com. If you would like a free introductory copy of the Messies Anonymous quarterly newsletter, send a self-addressed, stamped envelope to the address above.

Another source of help and information is the National Study Group on Chronic Disorganization. This group will be especially helpful if you or a family member has been diagnosed with

Attention Deficit Disorder (ADD). For more information or a reading list, contact the National Study Group on Chronic Disorganization, 1142 Chatsworth Drive, Avondale Estates, GA 30002; (404) 231-6172.

ON-LINE ORGANIZING SERVICES

If you don't have a professional organizer near you or if you just need a little help getting started, try Let's Get It Together, an on-line consulting service at http://freeweb.pdq.net/bman. On-line organizing services include:

- Establishing a bill-paying system
- Managing paper flow
- Storage solutions (single room or entire house)
- Time management
- Special projects

During your initial E-mail consultation (free), your consultant will help you determine your single biggest organizing challenge. Then, during the next three E-mail discussions, your consultant will help you create and personalize the best organizing plan for your home.

Or take an on-line class in getting organized. Go to http://getolife.hypermart. net and click on on-line class.

Step 3

Lighten Your Load

In this chapter . . .

- *How Much Is Enough?*
- *Getting Started*
- *Throw It Away*
- *Games People Play*
- *Places to Donate*
- *It Pays to Unclutter*

If you start panicking at the mere thought of getting rid of stuff, relax. Lightening your load doesn't mean throwing everything out. What it does mean is getting rid of things you don't use or love, so that you'll have more space and time for more important things.

Many people describe the process of paring down their belongings as liberating — even energizing. You'll never know until you try it! These same people say that you might think you'll miss these things, but you won't. You also won't miss all those frantic searches through cluttered closets, boxes, and stacks of paper.

How Much Is Enough?

Do you really need 23 pair of shoes? Or seven sets of sheets for your bed? Or that handy-dandy gadget you just saw advertised on television? How many things that you have bought are still in your home, but not being used?

Acquiring things has become such a habit that we often don't think about the cost of acquisition. Think about the price you pay — not just the cost of purchasing, but the cost of owning. On a practical level, your belongings cost you storage space and they cost you the time it takes to care for them. The more you own, the more you have to care for. If you're charging purchases and carrying balances on your credit cards, you're paying a lot more than the item is worth, even if you buy it on sale. Which is more painful — not having the latest widget or looking at your credit-card bill every month? You also pay the price of time spent shopping, and while you can buy many things, you can't buy time.

Much of what we own was bought, consciously or subconsciously, to project an image of success. Wouldn't you rather be recognized for who you are and what you have accomplished instead of what you own?

No matter how much you acquire, you will never have it all. Better to have a few possessions that you love and use than a thousand that weigh you down.

⁓

If you really want to lighten your load, what you need to do is figure out what is enough in your life and get rid of the rest. Albany, NY–based professional organizer Helen Volk asks her clients the following key question to determining how much is enough: On a scale of ten to one, with ten being everything you currently own and zero being nothing, what would feel more reasonable? Nine? Eight? Seven? Six? Five? If five seems about right, then you might consider eliminating about 50 percent of your belongings.

⁓

In the *Simple Living Journal* (Winter 1998), Julie Moss Scandora advises, "As you pare down your possessions, pare down the activities." Constant activity just adds to the clutter.

⁓

For ideas and inspiration for living a better life with less stuff, The Yearning for Balance Action Kit ($10) helps people establish new buying guidelines and find alternatives to recreational shopping. The kit is available from The Center for a New American Dream, 6930 Carroll Avenue, Suite 900, Takoma Park, MD 20912.

Getting Started

There's no right way to unclutter and no one way that works for everyone. What's important to remember is that getting started is far more important than how you get started!

Figure out where to start. Begin by taking that first step.

Start with the easy stuff. This will get you into the act of uncluttering with little or no pain or anxiety. Get a large garbage bag and walk through your house. Throw out anything that is clearly garbage:

- Expired medicines
- Expired coupons
- Outdated clothes
- Makeup that's more than one year old
- Sunscreen that's more than two years old
- Things that are broken unless they are valuable and fixable
- Odd socks
- Grocery bags (10 is enough)
- Old restaurant and shopping guides
- Outdated calendars
- Spoiled food
- Rusted utensils and tools
- Travel literature and maps (unless they are new and you have definite plans to travel in the next three months)

Start with a single drawer or shelf. Empty the contents, so you can see everything. Pick up each item and make a decision. If you haven't used or needed that item in the last year or simply don't like or want it anymore, put it in a bag. When you're done, put the bag in the trash. If possible, do this on trash night so you won't be tempted to retrieve anything. Continue to tackle one drawer or one shelf every day. This is the s-l-o-w but steady approach. It's like cutting out one soda, or 100 hundred calories a day. In a year, you'll have lost 10 pounds . . . painlessly.

Another easy way to get started is to sort things into the rooms where they belong. Go into any room with a laundry basket or large box. Put into it all the things that don't belong in that room. Take these things to the rooms in which they do belong and put them in the places where they belong. Socks, for example, should get put away in your sock drawer. (Don't worry about organizing the drawer. Once you've got the rest of the room in order, you might have the time or motivation to organize your sock drawer.) When you put away the last item, look around the room you are in. Put all things into the basket that don't belong in that room and then take them to where they do

There must be more to life than having everything!

— Maurice Sendak

belong. Repeat until all rooms contain only what belongs in those rooms. Now select one room on which to focus all of your attention.

⁓

Start by organizing your car or just the trunk. In as little as an hour or two, you can unclutter your car and know (perhaps for the first time ever) what it feels like to be organized. If you're really into it, wash your car and vacuum the interior. Imagine the surprise on the faces of your friends and family the next time they get into your car. By cleaning out your car, you'll get an idea of what it feels like to have your entire home clutter-free, and that feeling of pride and accomplishment will motivate you to keep working at it. Let the state of your car act as an early warning system. If it starts getting cluttered, you'll know that you need to focus more energy and attention on keeping your life clutter-free. (See the tips in step 7.)

⁓

Do not try to unclutter your whole house at once. Work in one room at a time and don't switch to another room until you're done. Seeing progress will motivate you to keep up the good work.

⁓

Plan on spending no more than one hour each day on uncluttering activities. After an hour, you won't be so fresh, and your decision-making ability may falter.

Commit to spending at least 20 to 30 minutes uncluttering each day.

Start out fresh. Don't start out tired from your day at work.

Start by uncluttering your kitchen or living room so you can comfortably host unexpected guests.

Ask a friend or family member for help and offer your help or services in return.

Close all cabinet, cupboard, and closet doors. It's amazing how much neater it makes a room.

While you're tackling the months and years of accumulated stuff, try to stay current with today's stuff. Open, sort, and file mail daily. Hang up your clothes when you take them off. Clean up the kitchen every night after dinner. And for every new thing you bring in the front door, send five items packing out the back door until you get your belongings down to a more manageable level.

If frustration or lack of time gets the best of you, find a receptacle for your stuff (a box, a closet, or a room) and close the lid or door. You can come back to it another day.

Make and commit to a daily plan. Set simple goals such as "Tonight, I'm going to clean out my junk drawer and then I'm going to stop." Or "I'm going to clean up for 20 minutes and then I'm going to stop." Then do it.

Finish what you're doing before you move on. To avoid getting sidetracked, make a note to remind yourself of things you want to do later like organizing your sock drawer or your photographs. (See step 6 for tips on "Schedules, Lists, and Notes.")

Throw It Away

As you decide the relative merit of each item, ask yourself the following questions:

- When was the last time I used this?
- Why don't I use it more often?
- Does it have any sentimental value?
- Do I love it?
- What is the worst possible thing that could happen if I just threw it away?
- Could I get another one if I needed to?
- If I keep it, where should it go? How many of these do I need?

Most of the stuff we save is pretty easily replaced. Five years from now, you might wish you still had that fondue pot, but if you need something only once every five years, you can probably borrow it from a friend. Or do without it.

If the idea of going through your house deciding what to throw out is unnerving, think instead in terms of deciding what you're going to keep. Keep those things you use or love and let go of the rest.

In the words of Ralph Waldo Emerson, "Always do what you are afraid to do."

When uncluttering a shelf, drawer, cupboard, or closet, take everything out. If you pick and choose things, you'll barely make a dent. Put like things together. Eliminate what you don't use, contain what's left, and put it back.

When uncluttering your clothes closet, take everything out and lay it on a bed. Vacuum your closet before putting anything back. Decide item by item what you will put back. Only keep what you use! (You may want to set aside a full morning for this project so you can finish what you start.)

Get three boxes and a large garbage bag. Label the boxes "give away or sell," "put away," and "store." As you sort through your belongings, put items in the appropriate box. The bag is for throwing away what you determine to be garbage. As you fill up each "give away" box, tape it shut so you won't tempted to look in it. You'll just have to make the same decisions over again. (You can use paper bags instead of boxes if you prefer. Fill them about halfway, and then fold over the top and staple it shut. Write "give away" on the bag.) Get rid of these boxes or bags right away. It really doesn't matter where you take them. Just get them out of the house.

Before you tie up each garbage bag, toss in your worries and fears and get rid of the emotional garbage that's cluttering your life!

If the thought of throwing some things out makes you uncomfortable, put those things in a box. If you haven't opened it in six months, throw the whole box out! Don't even open it. You haven't missed those things because you don't need them. Get rid of them!

Plan uncluttering activities around garbage days or plan to take stuff to the dump or your selected charity that day. Otherwise, you may be tempted to reconsider.

Ideally, you will move boxes and storage bins to where they will be stored. If you have to create a temporary holding place until you can clean out the permanent area, make it somewhere that's out of your way.

Think of keeping things this way: For each item you keep, you are sacrificing space. Is it worth the space it occupies, or could that space be better used to store something else or to create breathing space?

~

Sandra Felton, author of numerous books for "messies" and founder of Messies Anonymous, says, "Be willing to take a risk that you may want later what you discarded. Also realize that it may cause temporary pain to throw something out. However, it also causes definite pain to keep it. Throwing it out is mild pain, compared with the pain which comes from having to live helplessly with all the clutter which finds its way into the house."

~

Do it when the mood strikes.

~

Do it when you're angry.

~

Make decisions quickly.

~

Never think back.

~

Cultivate a healthy attitude. Don't think of uncluttering as getting rid of stuff. Think of it as giving it to someone who needs it more than you. Or think of it as recycling. Either way, you will feel doubly good.

By all means, if something holds a great deal of sentimental value and you absolutely cannot part with it, don't!

~

Have a friend or family member who knows your style help you determine what clothes to keep.

~

If you are afraid to let go of something, do it scared. You may find that overcoming your fear of letting go of material possessions will help you overcome other fears as well. In fact, the act of letting go can trigger a release of frustration, anger, guilt, and other emotional garbage.

~

Clean out one drawer each night. You will make progress toward your goal each day and it won't seem like such a huge project.

~

Ask yourself these questions: Is this something I truly like? Do I use it? Will I need it in the near future? Would I have trouble getting a new one if I had to? If not, throw it out.

~

If you are clearing away years and years of accumulated junk, consider calling a dump runner to haul it away. They price by job and it's less expensive than a roll-off container. They'll even carry out all your boxes for a fee.

Few rich men own their property.
The property owns them.

— Robert G. Ingersoll

On trash night, go through your refrigerator and throw out food that's moldy or past the expiration date. When in doubt, throw it out.

Be careful how you dispose of hazardous materials. These include paints, solvents, pesticides, motor oil, batteries, oven cleaners, and other household products. Improper disposal can cause serious pollution and health problems. For information on how to dispose of hazardous materials, call your local municipality.

If you live in the city, put stuff out at the curb (furniture, recycling). You'll be surprised at what disappears overnight. Call the city for a pickup of whatever's left.

Games People Play

Because we tend to attach personal meaning to our belongings, it's common to perform divestment rituals to remove the meaning before selling them or giving them away. You might, for instance, feel you need to wash or dry-clean clothing before donating it. Don't try to downplay the emotional attachment to your things. Some people find it helps to take photographs of possessions they wish to remember.

Break large tasks into smaller tasks.

Pretend you're going on vacation and you have to get everything done before you go. You'll be surprised at how much you can get done in that mode.

Imagine that you're moving. Ask yourself: Is this item worth the effort of packing up, carrying out to the moving van, and unpacking at the new place? If not, give it a new home.

Work to music. Turn on the radio or put on a CD. Plan to work for only two or three songs.

Uncluttering can help you lighten up in more ways than one. As you move around your home cleaning up clutter, make it aerobic. Push yourself to move as quickly as you can — fast enough that you can hear yourself breathing. A half-hour of making beds, climbing stairs, putting away laundry, and other fast-paced uncluttering activities can burn up to 150 calories, depending on your weight. So go ahead and lighten up!

FRIENDS, ACQUAINTANCES, STRANGERS

Judith Kolberg, Director of the National Study Group on Chronic Disorganization, believes that we have a tendency to imbue inanimate objects with human emotions. She asks her clients, "Does this item need you?" rather than "Do you need this item?"

In her work with people who are chronically disorganized, Kolberg emphasizes the emotional attachment to our possessions in a game she calls Friends, Acquaintances, and Strangers. You can play this game with nearly all of your belongings — from clothing to books, jewelry to furniture. Let's say you are getting ready to unclutter your clothes closet. As you look at each item, ask yourself if it is a friend, an acquaintance, or a stranger.

You love and need your friends. So an outfit you wear often is obviously a friend. Acquaintances, on the other hand, have a habit of appearing out of nowhere and often overstay their welcome. Something you bought but never wore would be an acquaintance. It's time to find these things a new home. Clothes that don't fit or that you haven't worn in a year or more are strangers. You don't want strangers in your house, do you? Kick out the strangers. Also kick out accessories that belong with clothing you no longer own.

Think positive. You are an optimist, aren't you? Otherwise, how could you keep going every day despite the clutter?

Organize a cleaning party. Find a few people who are willing to help you in return for helping them. Plan to spend one Saturday at each house. It's amazing how much you can accomplish with a little help.

Washington, D.C.–based professional organizer Gloria Ritter tries to hold each item as her client decides what to do with it, because holding an item increases your attachment to that object. It's precisely this reason that a good salesperson will encourage you to touch something or try it on! Ask a friend to help you decide what to keep and what to toss by holding each item for you.

To make a decision about keeping something, decide if you want to be that object's caretaker any longer. Or is it time to give that job to someone with more time and space for it?

As you pare down your belongings, give thanks for all that has enabled you to have such abundance in your life. Then share your wealth.

Use the ABC system for sorting clothes. Take everything out of your closet. Separate clothes into three piles: A, B, and C. The A pile is for clothes you wear and like and definitely want to keep. The B pile is for things you might keep. The C pile is for things that you haven't worn in more than a year or that don't fit. Put the A pile away. Then go through the B pile again. Donate clothes in the C pile.

Set a timer. A ticking timer is best because it keeps you focused on your task. Allow 10 minutes at the end of each cleanup session to put things where they belong. Don't worry about organizing them right now. Just put them away.

When you finish cleaning out an area or your time is up, put away your boxes and start again tomorrow.

Places to Donate

If you have things that are still in good condition, consider donating them rather than throwing them away. If you itemize on your income taxes, don't forget to get a receipt for your tax-deductible donations.

The Salvation Army and other organizations that run thrift shops will accept a wide variety of items ranging from furniture and household goods to clothing and shoes.

If you call, The Salvation Army may come to your house and pick up donations — for free — and send you a receipt. Just make sure that what you leave for pickup is clearly marked, so they don't accidentally take something you intended to keep!

If your church is having a rummage sale, bring everything there.

Police stations, hospitals, and children's homes will accept clean toys in good condition.

Libraries will accept used books.

Women's shelters are always in need of household goods, bedding, towels, and women's and children's clothing to give families a new start.

A senior citizen's center or center for persons with disabilities may be able to use unused fabric.

Complete possession is proved only by giving. All you are unable to give possesses you.

— André Gide

It Pays to Unclutter

You can throw away or give away things you no longer use or need, or you can sell them. For many people, selling off things feels better than just throwing stuff away. You won't get rich uncluttering your house, but you may end up with anywhere from $10 to several hundred dollars — enough to treat yourself to a little fun. Following are just a few ideas of ways to reward yourself for eliminating the junk in and around your home.

- Take yourself and a friend out to lunch.
- Get a professional manicure or pedicure.
- Go away for the weekend.
- Start a vacation fund.
- Send flowers to someone for no reason at all.
- Buy flowers for yourself.
- Make a charitable donation.
- Order take-out Chinese food for dinner.

Now, for some tips on getting cash for things you no longer use or need . . .

Advertise larger items like furniture, appliances, power tools, or computer equipment in your local newspaper.

Have a garage or yard sale. Take out a classified ad and be sure to list your big-ticket items.

Sell books, clothing, and furniture on consignment. At a secondhand or consignment shop, you generally get 40 to 50 percent of the selling price. You sign a contract for 60 days, after which you have 10 days to come back in and pick up whatever didn't sell, along with a check for what did sell.

If it's too late in the season to bring in your clothes, put them in storage and put a note in your tickler file (see step 6) to get them out before the beginning of the next season.

SELLING CLOTHING ON CONSIGNMENT

Clothes must be in excellent condition with no loose or missing buttons, no falling hems or tears in the material, no stains. Newer clothes, designer names, and classic styles sell best. If you happen to have some vintage classic clothes, take them to a vintage clothes store. Usually, stores request that clothes be brought in ready to sell; i.e., cleaned, pressed, and on hangers.

The best time to bring seasonal clothes to a consignment shop:

Spring/summer	Mid-February
Fall	Mid-August
Winter	End of September/ early October

Items accepted on consignment include:

- Clothing
- Hats, belts, handbags, and accessories
- Shoes and boots
- Jewelry
- Decorative household items
- Furniture
- Books

There are even consignment shops for kid's stuff. Bring in toys, baby equipment, videos, books, children's sports equipment (no stuffed animals, no cardboard puzzles, and no games).

A pawnbroker will give you cash for all kinds of items including:

- Tools
- Stamps and coins
- Electronics
- Computers
- China
- Antiques
- Jewelry
- Diamonds
- Gold and silver
- Musical instruments

If you have items you think might be antiques and you don't want them, take them to an antiques dealer. Don't feel you have to keep antiques just because they're antiques. Keep them because you love them. Antiques could include:

- Toys
- Jewelry
- Dolls
- Furniture
- Glassware
- Military items
- Paintings
- Clocks
- Lamps
- Watches
- Fine china
- Photographs
- Books
- Bicycles

ON-LINE SELLING AND BARTERING

Trade or sell anything you don't want at the Barter Station on the Internet. Go to http://www.solutions-4U.com and click on Barter Station. You could barter your wedding dress, jewelry, power equipment, baby furniture, or anything else of value.

Contain Yourself

In this chapter . . .

- *Storage Basics*
- *Favorite Organizing Products*
- *Seasonal Storage*
- *Space-Saving Storage*
- *Inexpensive Storage*
- *Photographs*
- *Kid's Stuff*

Y ou've heard this before: A place for everything and everything in its place. Having a place for everything saves time, work, and frustration. Until you designate a place for things, you just keep moving clutter from one place to another. Find a place for everything. Keep things near where you use them and then always put them back.

As you begin to think about storage, remember that your goal is to lighten your load and then contain what's left. What you want to avoid is bringing in more stuff just to organize your stuff. That defeats the purpose of uncluttering.

In reality, containing stuff falls short of concealing the fact that we all have too much stuff. Regular purging means less stuff to contain.

Storage Basics

Decide how long you will keep things and how much space you will allocate for storage. When it seems like it's time to add more storage space, it's probably time to eliminate some stuff.

Keep like items together. You may do this already by piling like items in similar piles. Hey! You've got the right idea!

Store things where you use them.

Label everything. Use wide, felt-tip markers to write on labels and place labels where they can be seen easily from a distance. Store boxes and bins with labels facing out so you can find what you're looking for without having to move heavy boxes.

Store the things you use most often in the most accessible places.

When organizing your clothes, look for patterns — amount of usage, colors, season — and group items according to whatever pattern suits you.

Keep an open catchall box in your storage area for catching all those things you find throughout the year that belong in one of the packed boxes. Instead of getting everything out just to put away one item, keep it in the "catchall" box. Next time you pull out all the boxes, put away the things in the catchall box.

Store things you use only once a year or less in the back or bottom of your storage area. Store more frequently used items in the front or on top.

Use storage bins with different color lids to store things; for example, a green lid for holiday decorations and blue for spring/summer clothes.

If you own your home, consider adding built-in storage. You'll appreciate it for as long as you live there and if you decide to sell, the storage will add value to your home.

Keep a master storage list. Update the list when you add to or retrieve an item from storage. Assign a code to each container and then write on a 3×5 card what is stored in each container. For example, J1 = Judy's stuff; container #1 contains winter outerwear: scarves, hats, gloves, and boots.

INDEXING STORAGE

If you prepare your master storage list using spreadsheet software, you can print a master list and sort by item and containers.

Favorite Organizing Products

Half the job of organizing is having the right tools. There are some terrific products you can buy to help organize your possessions. But remember . . . for every one thing you buy, something must go and that goes for organizing products, too! Be careful that you're not just organizing clutter. You want to keep it pared down.

If you do not have any clear plastic storage bins with lids, go out and get some. If you only have one or two, go get some more. Organized and disorganized people alike swear by these bins. Disorganized people hide stuff in them just to get it out of sight, which is a start. Organized people use them to store everything from puzzle pieces to scuba-diving equipment and craft supplies to holiday decorations. What makes these bins so popular is:

- They're clear so you can see at a glance what's inside.
- They come in lots of different sizes.
- They're stackable.
- They're watertight so you can store things in the basement or garage without worrying about them getting wet.
- They keep out dust and dirt.
- They're fairly inexpensive and go on sale several times a year.
- They're readily available at mass-merchandise stores.

For storing blankets, comforters, sweaters, and other seasonal clothing, vacuum storage bags are a space-saving alternative to plastic storage bins. You simply use a vacuum hose to compress air within the bag.

Hat boxes, decorative tins, and woven baskets are wonderful for hiding or organizing clutter while adding to the decor of the room.

Furniture with built-in storage is attractive and functional. Look for trunk-style coffee tables, beds with drawers underneath, and covered benches with room to store hats, scarves, mittens, knapsacks, gym bags, and whatever.

Bike-rack poles that extend from floor to ceiling and require no mounting are great for apartment dwellers.

Sometimes, the best organizing product is something you have in your home that you acquired for some other purpose. A magnetic knife holder can be used in the bathroom to hold nail clippers, tweezers, and scissors. One woman found that a silver toast holder made a decorative mail sorter for her desk.

Hanging shoe bags take up less space than standing shoe racks, especially if you can hang them over the back of a door. They can also be used for storing sewing supplies, crafts, tools, bean bag toys, and more. Use a hanging shoe bag as a magazine "rack" in your bathroom. Hang one behind the front seat of your car to store children's toys. Or use a hanging shoe bag to store cleaning supplies in a closet.

Seasonal Storage

If you have kids, you probably celebrate even minor holidays with as much gusto as you do the major ones. What do you do with the half-used roll of Valentine tissue paper? Or the Halloween cups and napkins that are left over? It doesn't make sense to toss these things, but you want to be able to find them.

One mother of two bought six large, covered plastic tubs — one for each holiday — and decorated the outside to identify the holiday. Now that every holiday has its assigned home, it's much easier to keep and find decorations.

Store holiday decoration boxes in order by date and then rotate as the holiday passes.

Wrap holiday tree lights around wrapping-paper tubes to keep them free of tangles.

Organize holiday tree decorations in layers in big boxes in the order that you put them on your tree.

Store small, breakable tree ornaments in empty egg cartons.

Store bows, ribbon, and wrapping paper in a drawer or bin, along with decorations for the appropriate holiday.

Keep year-round wrapping paper in an accessible bin or drawer. Store scissors and tape in there, too.

Limit yourself to one or two kinds of wrapping paper and one or two colors of ribbon and bows that will work for everything. A pretty pastel print can be used for showers and weddings; a brightly colored print makes a fine wrap for birthday presents for children, men, and women.

To keep wrapping paper from unwrapping itself, cut a slit from end to end in an empty wrapping tube and slide it over the new roll. It also makes it easier to dispense paper when you need it.

Put bows and ribbon in a plastic storage bag and use a clothespin to attach the bag to a hanger.

Cover hanging decorations with plastic garbage bags, tape closed, and hang from the rafters in your basement, garage, or attic.

Out-of-season clothes are best kept inside the main part of the house in another closet.

If you don't have a cedar chest or closet for storing winter woolens, place them in a large trash bag, add a small plastic bag that has been pierced and filled with mothballs, squeeze excess air out of the bag, and secure with a twist tie.

If you must store seasonal clothes in the basement or garage, put them in a large plastic storage bin or garbage can labeled "Seasonal Storage."

Store children's clothing in boxes labeled by age or size and sex.

Space-Saving Storage

Think vertical. There's always unused vertical space in any given room. Floor-to-ceiling shelving is a perfect example of space-saving storage.

If you store things up high, keep a step stool handy. If you don't have one, get one. You'll wonder how you ever lived without it.

Hanging tiered baskets can be used to sort mail. Use one tier for incoming mail for other members of the house, one for outgoing mail, and one for bills.

If you don't have a linen closet, store linens in plastic bins, boxes, or zippered vinyl bags under each bed. Or use this space to store luggage.

Use the space between the refrigerator and wall to hang your dustpan and broom.

Install closet organizers in every closet.

Use the back of every door of every room, closet, and cabinet. Hang wire shelving or a shoe bag, or add a few clothes hooks.

Use a wheeled filing cabinet that can double as a nightstand or buffet with a pretty tablecloth thrown over it.

Inexpensive Storage

Use empty baby wipe containers in medicine cabinets to separate and store first-aid supplies, makeup, pain relievers, and vitamins.

To store odds and ends in the kitchen junk drawer, workshop, or kids' rooms, use recycled microwave food trays, checkbook boxes, or margarine tubs.

Instead of buying storage bins for items you use regularly, buy dishpans. If you fill them only three-quarters full, you can stack them pretty well.

Check out your local dollar store for inexpensive jewelry organizers and shoe bags.

To make quick and easy shelving, lay boards across bricks or glass or concrete blocks to support heavy loads, or use clay flowerpots or painted coffee cans between boards for medium-weight loads.

Plastic milk crates make terrific organizers. You can stack them face out against a wall and use them to store books, binders, and notebooks.

Use cardboard copy-paper boxes from work or get them from a copy store.

Cardboard produce boxes with lids make sturdy storage boxes, and they're free.

Wooden produce boxes stack nicely for storage just about anywhere, and they're also free.

I'LL DRINK TO THAT

Liquor cartons have many uses for organizing. You can roll up artwork and store it in the partitions. Or wrap holiday ornaments in tissue or newspaper and store several in each partition. These boxes also come in handy in the workshop for storing short lengths of molding, furring strips, or metal rods. Use one in your coat closet to store dry umbrellas. To store long-handled garden tools, cut the bottoms from two boxes, stack on top of a third, and tape together.

Empty egg cartons can be quite useful. Remove the lid from one and place it in a desk drawer to hold paper clips and other small items. Or use one to store rings and other jewelry. (See "Seasonal Storage" in this chapter and "Kids' Rooms" in step 5 for more ways to use egg cartons.)

The tops of aerosol cans can be used as drawer organizers. They're great for containing paper clips, screws, and nails.

Shoe boxes make very sturdy, multifunctional storage containers. Use a shoe box to store photos, or as a drawer organizer.

Film canisters are very useful for storing small items like buttons and safety pins or screws and nails for your toolbox. Use masking tape to label each container or use a piece of clear tape to attach a sample item to the outside of the container. (See "Organizing to Go" in step 6 for more ways to use film canisters.)

Photographs

Gather all photographs together in one spot. Schedule some time each week to put photographs into albums until you are done.

If you haven't been putting photos into albums, the easiest way to get started is to start a new album with your most recent photographs and continue from there.

It's nice to have photographs in yearly albums, but it's difficult to go back through years and years of photos and figure out when they were taken. It might be easier to create a family album for family photos, and a vacation album for vacation photos.

Start a new photo album for each new child or grandchild.

If you really dislike putting photographs in albums, file them in shoe boxes, clear plastic boxes, or photo boxes with indexed dividers.

There are only two ways to avoid photograph clutter: (1) Don't take any photographs, or (2) put photographs into albums immediately. Keep albums easily accessible.

Immediately throw away any photos that did not develop properly. There is absolutely no reason to save them except to take them back to the developer. (Some developers give credit for improperly developed film, regardless if it was the fault of the photographer or the developer.)

Memorabilia boxes are a great way to save your most precious mementos — love letters, cards, baby items. Limit boxes to one per person.

ON-LINE PHOTOS

Some developers now offer the option of getting your film delivered on-line or storing photos electronically. This allows you the opportunity to print only the photos you want. And it eliminates the need to file. You can share your photos instantly with friends and family via the Web or E-mail, enhance photos using photo-editing software, and order reprints and enlargements. The photos can be used to create customized greeting cards, letters — even school projects. For a demonstration, visit http://www.kodak.photonet.com.

Consider keeping all formal portraits (baby, school, wedding, family) in a formal family album. If you have enough prints, you could put several of these albums together and give them as gifts.

~

Use an accordion-style file with labeled folders to sort photographs into different categories, such as vacations, sporting events, celebrations, and family, or however you want to organize them. Save only the best photographs and throw out the rest.

~

Consider labeling photographs with name, date, location, and details that may be meaningful 10 years from now when you're not sure where the photo was taken or who is in it.

~

To keep negatives from deteriorating, use three-ring plastic sheets divided into strip openings (available at most photo shops). Label each sheet with the month and year. Place chronologically in three-ring binders and label each binder spine chronologically.

~

If you're not too concerned about preservation, keep negatives in the original envelopes from the processor and store in shoe boxes, each labeled with dates chronologically (i.e., 1995–1997).

When you need to replace your camera, consider getting one of the new cameras that use Kodak Advantix film. This film gives you a thumbnail print before printing all of the photographs, so you can develop only those photographs you want.

Kids' Stuff

Go to your local pizza store and ask for a couple of clean pizza boxes — one for each child. Write the child's name on the box, and use it to store a year's worth of school papers and artwork. Kids can keep their art boxes under their beds. Make it their responsibility to "file" everything they bring home.

If you pick up your children from school, keep paper-towel or wrapping-paper tubes in the car for rolling up artwork. For those pieces you wish to save, write your child's name on the outside of the tube along with the date.

Fold (if necessary) and punch artwork to fit a three-ring binder. Create one binder for each child. At the end of the year, save one or two favorites.

Set up a file folder for each child's schoolwork. Purge at the end of the year.

Periodically purge when the kids are asleep.

Place children's art in scrapbooks labeled with their names. Include artwork, notes from school, report cards, exceptional schoolwork, and school photos.

If you have room in a closet, use a cardboard dresser to store artwork and mementos. Assign one or two drawers to each child.

Recycle your children's artwork. Choose your favorites each year to create special gift calendars. Create the calendar pages on your computer and then have the artwork and calendar pages laminated and spiral-bound by an office-supply store.

Take photos of your child with some of his or her favorite outfits, toys, scout uniform, or projects. Put the photos in your photo album and throw out the mementos.

You can also take photos of artwork, keeping only your favorite pieces.

When considering where to keep children's artwork and schoolwork, keep in mind that it should be easily accessible. One father found that by moving a few tapes under the VCR, he created an empty spot to store those papers.

Revamp
Clutter Zones

In this chapter . . .

- *The Big Picture*
- *Entranceways*
- *Closets and Drawers*
- *Kids' Rooms*
- *Bathroom*
- *Bedroom*
- *Kitchen and
  Dining Room*

- *Family Room and
  Living Room*
- *Home Office*
- *Basement, Attic,
  and Garage*
- *Tools, Hobbies, and
  Sports Equipment*
- *Car Interiors*

O rganizing your home and possessions to fit
your lifestyle can go a long way toward
minimizing clutter while making better
use of your space. The key is to work with clutter
instead of against it.

Where do you tend to drop your keys when you come in the door? Where do you put things you need to take with you when you leave for work? Where do you sort bills? Where do you do most of your reading? These are the most logical places for you to contain your things.

Walk through your home and look at what's lying around. Consider how you use each room. Ask these questions:

- What causes clutter in this room?
- What items end up here that should be somewhere else?
- What things should be in this room that are not here now?
- What kind of storage could I use here?

Is your dining-room table or kitchen counter, for example, a dumping ground for anything and everything that comes in the door? Can you find or create a better place nearby to contain these things? Would better storage in your entranceway solve the problem?

The Big Picture

A very effective way to minimize clutter is to set up work centers for specific activities such as handling mail and bills, sewing, hobbies, and laundry. A workstation with all the tools you need close at hand makes you more efficient, so you save time.

If your hobbies are always taking up space in the kitchen, claim a corner and make it your space with a worktable and a cabinet designated for your supplies. If you lightened your load as described in step 3, it's possible that you now have a large closet somewhere that could become a hobby room or maybe even an office.

⁓

If you do not have a desk, get one or make a place where you can pay bills, write your to-do list or your shopping list, and write cards or letters to friends. Organize your desk with all the supplies you need: stationery, envelopes, pens, pencils, markers, paper clips, tape, scissors, postage stamps, and your personal address book or phone directory.

⁓

As you revamp clutter zones, consider creating your own personal sanctuary — a space you can call your own, where you can read or write or think in privacy. If you live with others and cannot claim an entire room for yourself, claim a portion of a room and declare it off-limits to everyone but yourself.

⁓

Evaluate the storage in every room. Good storage maximizes your space and provides easy access to the things you use most often. Look for invisible storage spots — you might be able to create a tool room under a staircase, or store linens in a box under your bed.

As you look at the arrangement of things in a particular room, think about the following questions to help you determine where each item belongs:

- How often do I use it?
- Where does it get used?
- How accessible is it? How accessible do I need it to be?
- Does this item have any special storage requirements?

If you have a place for storing particular things, but it isn't being used, figure out why. Perhaps it is not conveniently located. A good example is the hamper. If your kids get undressed in the bedroom, but the hamper is in the bathroom or the laundry room, it's no wonder their dirty clothes always wind up on the floor.

If you find you're always looking for things like scissors and tape, put these items in all of the locations where you need to use them.

If you live on two or more floors, leave a large basket with a handle at the bottom of your stairs to collect things that need to go up. When you go up the stairs, take the basket with you. Put items where they belong and leave the basket at the top of the stairs to bring back down with you. Do not leave items on the stairs where you or others could trip or slip on them.

Use a decorative screen or ceiling-to-floor roller blind to partition off a room and create a workstation or storage area.

Use a decorative screen to hide areas that look "cluttery." You can use this technique to hide shoes or bins in the hallway, portable filing cabinets in your office, or even a pile of stuff you just haven't had time to get to — yet!

It takes time to organize your home to fit you and your lifestyle. Give yourself the time to do it right. A quick solution might end up being just a quick fix.

Consider rearranging furniture, especially if everything's been in the same place for 10 years. When your surroundings are stale, you too become stale.

Unclutter your walls. Take down everything and put back only what you love in locations where you can enjoy looking at your favorite things.

Group collections together in one large display, rather than scattering items all over a room. This goes for photographs on the walls, too.

Entranceways

Your front entrance (or the entrance you use most frequently) creates the first impression of your home, which affects not only visitors, but also you and your family. What you see upon entering and leaving each day will have a subtle effect upon your mental state.

Feng shui practitioners believe this can ultimately affect your health and fortune. If the entrance to your home is cluttered, you are greeted each day with things that stand in the way of your goals. Clearing your front entrance of obstacles may allow you to clear the obstacles in your life.

A tendency to let clutter build near the doorway may also indicate resistance to going out into the world. Are you creating a barricade? What do you fear? Do you fear letting go of the familiar?

Move items that don't belong in the entryway to where they do belong.

If you don't have a coat closet, install coat pegs along one wall for coats and umbrellas.

Install a double coat hook for each child at a height low enough to hang jackets and backpacks.

Place a shoe rack or large wicker basket near the front door to collect shoes. When you always take off your shoes at the door, you'll always know where your shoes are, and your carpets and floors will stay cleaner.

~

In winter or wet weather, set out a large, flat pan or boot tray for wet shoes and boots.

~

To organize mittens and gloves, use a hanging shoe bag with clear plastic pockets. Hang it in your coat closet or behind the closet door. Or put hats and mittens in a wire basket on a closet shelf.

~

If you have children, create a "launchpad" area in a hall closet or along one wall of the hallway or kitchen. Stack plastic crates — one for each child — for collecting lunch boxes, graded homework and tests, announcements, and paperwork to be signed. Encourage them to put everything in their crates when they come home and to take everything out when they leave in the morning.

~

Hang a doorknob basket and use it to store keys and outgoing mail. You may also use a tiered wall basket or letter holder, or a decorative key hanger.

Closets and Drawers

Need more closet space for clothes? Get rid of what you never wear! (See step 3.)

Your goal is to make everything in every closet visible and accessible.

If your clothes closet has one bar and one shelf, no wonder you can't keep it organized! The closet organizer kits you can buy in department stores are fairly inexpensive and not too difficult to install yourself. If you're not at all handy and you can't get anyone to help you, or if you can afford it, call a company that will come in and do it for you. Look in the yellow pages under "Closets and Closet Accessories." You'll be amazed at how much more you can store and how much easier it is to find things.

Organize clothes by season. Keep out-of-season clothes at the back of your closet and rotate as the seasons change, or put them in another closet. If you haven't got a closet in which to hang out-of-season clothes, make a simple rack for hanging clothes in your basement by inserting a long pole between two step ladders. Cover several items with plastic garbage bags and tie a knot in the bottom of each bag.

Keep like items together. Hang long items with long items and short items with short items. Or hang pants together, skirts together, and blouses together. You might even arrange clothes by color from light to dark. Color-coding makes it easier to find a particular item of clothing.

Throw out all your wire hangers. Use only plastic, wooden, or padded hangers. Wire hangers do not properly support clothes and often bend or sag, resulting in a messy-looking closet, not to mention creases.

If you use plastic hangers, you can color-code clothing in any way that makes sense to you. For example, you can use three colors to divide clothes into casual, work, and dressy. Or if two or more people share a closet, you can assign one color hanger to each to make it easier to see where each individual's section begins and ends.

On the top shelf of your closet, use several wire baskets or plastic bins with lids for storing handbags, sweaters, or shoes.

If you have room in your closet, but not enough room in your drawers, install ventilated wire shelves and gliding drawers, a hanging garment bag with shelves, or a small dresser or clear plastic storage bin with drawers. Cardboard dressers are sturdy enough to use every day and come in many colors and prints.

To organize accessories, clip a couple of shower curtain rings to your clothes rod and use them to hang handbags, scarves, and belts. Or clip one ring around the top of a hanger and clip other rings onto it to make an accessory ladder that saves space. This is a great way to store umbrellas in a coat closet.

If there are certain accessories you always wear with a particular outfit, hang them with that outfit.

Organizing belts might be as simple as tapping a few hooks or nails into the back or side of your closet. Or you can roll them up and put them all in a plastic storage bin.

Make use of the inside of closet doors. On the back of a walk-in closet door, you can install a necktie or accessory rack, hang a shoebag, or install an accordion-style coat rack or hooks for hanging pajamas, nightgowns, and robes.

Shoe racks make good use of floor space and allow you to store many pairs in a small amount of space. Over-the-door shoe racks are also available.

If you want to keep shoes clean, especially seasonal or special-occasion shoes, save the original box or store them in clear plastic shoe boxes.

~

Store all dress shoes together, all work shoes together, and all play shoes together, or group them by color.

~

If you have trouble remembering what shoes are in which boxes, take a Polaroid picture of each pair of shoes and tape it to the box.

~

Use a plastic shoe bag with clear pouches to store pantyhose or socks.

~

Or store pantyhose in a large plastic storage bag attached to a wire hanger with a clothespin. If you have many pairs, separate them into light and dark colors and put them in two separate bags. By separating colors, you only have to search through half at a time.

~

If your closet space is very limited, try using tiered hangers for skirts and slacks that allow you to hang multiple items together. Another space-saving kind of hanger is the swing-out trouser rack. You'll find both types of hangers and many more closet organizing products in specialized mail-order catalogs (see the appendix), at most home centers, and in the housewares section at large department stores.

⁓

Hang extra bedspreads or blankets on hangers at the back of your clothes closet or from a rod on the back of your bedroom door.

⁓

Whether it's a clothes closet, linen closet, or hall closet, try to keep things off the floor. Hanging makes more efficient use of space.

⁓

If you haven't already, designate specific dresser drawers for specific items: socks and underwear, shirts, shorts, sweaters, and workout clothes.

⁓

Fold or roll socks. Don't ball them up because it causes them to lose their elasticity over time.

⁓

Drawer organizers make it easier to find things in your "underwear" drawer. Make your own by cutting down shoe boxes.

⁓

In linen closets, put washcloths and bath towels where they are most convenient for everyone — on a shelf at waist level. Put sheets on the next shelf up and other things like tablecloths and seasonal bedspreads on the highest shelves.

Instead of storing towels and sheets separately on a shelf, store them as sets. Wrap up the fitted sheet and pillowcases with the flat sheet, or place the sheets inside one pillowcase. Wrap up washcloths and hand towels with the bath towel. When you need a new set, you can just grab it with one hand.

~

If you store towels and sheets in stacks, store them folded side out to make it easier to grab just the ones you want.

~

Store an extra set of sheets and pillowcases between the mattress and box spring of each bed. When it's time to change sheets, the clean set is right there. It works best if you fold them in half and then several times lengthwise.

~

If you don't have a linen closet, but you do have some room in a closet with a clothes rod, hang towels and sheets on hangers. Fold washcloths, hand towels, bath towels, and bath mats once lengthwise and hang towel sets together on one hanger. You can store sheet sets this way, too, and even tablecloths.

~

Keep table linens from creasing by installing a rod beneath one shelf and hanging them on hangers padded with paper towel tubes. Just slice the tube lengthwise and roll it over the straight edge of the hanger.

To organize and store holiday tablecloths, hang an over-the-door towel rod on the inside of your linen closet. Use the paper towel tube trick from the previous tip to prevent creases.

Put old bookcases into closets for instant shelving.

Use a hanging shoe bag in your cleaning closet to hold cleaning supplies.

Organize your supply closet by keeping things like pet supplies (shampoo, flea powder, brushes) and shoe polishes together in clear plastic boxes. It's so nice to be able to open a single box and find everything you need in it without having to search all over.

Kids' Rooms

Let kids have input on organizing their rooms. Let them help you answer the following questions:

- Does everything in this room need to be stored here or could we store some things elsewhere?
- What do you like about how your things are stored? Is it easy or hard to put things away?
- What could be better?
- What are you no longer using that we could give away?

A proven technique for organizing toys is to use shelves wherever possible instead of boxes. Things tend to get thrown into boxes and broken or buried. With shelves, kids can see at a glance what's there.

Make it easy for children to put things away. That means having coat hooks at kid height, low shelves, and easily accessible storage bins.

Install hooks or pegs on the back of the door at child height for hanging backpacks and sleepwear.

Make it impossible for younger children to get at toys with small parts. Store these items high on shelves.

Store special toys like a marionette, model airplane, music box, china doll, or tea set in special places, so that children have to ask for the item.

When children are very young, keep toys where they are convenient for you.

Give kids an assortment of cigar and shoe boxes for collecting small things.

If dirty laundry never seems to make it to the hamper, put a hamper in your children's rooms. A large basket or colorful plastic trash can with a lid works well.

If you want kids to hang up their clothes, put hanging rods within their reach. To make an inexpensive, child-height clothes rod, run a length of chain through a piece of sturdy plastic pipe that will accommodate hangers. Attach each end of the chain to a shower curtain ring and hang the rings over the original clothes rod.

Or install a tension rod in the closet at the right height for hanging clothes and raise it as the child grows taller.

CREATE A CLOSET

Make a child-size closet out of a wooden chest with a hinged top. Simply screw legs into one end, which will become the bottom of the closet. Stand the chest up, put a rod across the inside and a knob or pull on the door. For safety reasons, use a friction catch instead of a locking device to keep the door closed.

When you buy children's clothes, ask to have the child-size hanger. It's so much easier to hang small clothes on small hangers.

Tape pictures or photographs of what goes in each dresser drawer to the outside or bottom of drawers, so even very young children can put clothes away. As they are learning to read, you can replace the pictures with words.

Hang matching outfits together in closets and fold matching outfits together in drawers for children who cannot coordinate colors.

Double drawer space with a sturdy, four-drawer cardboard dresser. If there's room, put it in the closet.

Put stackable crates in the closet or design a kid's closet with ventilated wire shelving that can be adjusted as he or she grows.

Create cubbyholes for books, toys, and games with colorful, stacking milk crates. Interlocking crates are best, but you can secure plain crates to each other using twist ties or clear packing tape.

Use hanging shoe bags on the back of a door or in the closet to store bean-bag toys, fashion dolls and clothes, cars, and other small things. Hang it low enough so that kids can reach into even the top pockets.

Label and use clear plastic shoe boxes for all kinds of things.

Limit what gets stored under the bed to those things that are in containers: storage bins, zippered bags, or shoe boxes.

What to do when puzzle boxes begin to disintegrate? Designate and label a plastic storage bin for puzzles. Cut out the picture and store it (folded, if necessary) with the puzzle pieces in a plastic bag.

Use the method described above for storing game pieces and instructions. Place in a plastic storage bin that's large enough to hold game boards as well.

Use empty egg cartons to store game pieces. Label one carton for each game, secure the lid with a rubber band and put it in the game box.

A time-saving idea for game storage is to put pieces in recycled margarine tubs and write the name of the game on each one. Stack them on a shelf. Write the name of the game on the back of each game board along one side of the spine or in one corner, fold and stack the game boards. If necessary, put instructions inside the folded board.

Store thin books and coloring books in magazine boxes. You can make your own using cereal boxes sliced on the diagonal.

Bookcases with doors are great for hiding a kid's clutter.

For inexpensive clutter control, buy a bunch of dishpans for organizing toys on shelves. Give one to each child.

Put a limit on toys. Children get more use out of their toys when they have fewer of them. And they tend to get more creative, making up games.

Designate and label a specific spot in children's rooms for everything. Tape a little picture of the toy in its spot. This is educational for toddlers, as it helps them with memory and matching skills.

Use small shoe boxes to catch Matchbox cars, action figures, and small plastic toys.

⌒

Organize toys in clear plastic bins by theme (for example, building blocks, cars, animals). The clear plastic allows kids to see what's inside at a glance. Very young children may need help opening the lids, which helps parents teach the practice of getting out one toy at a time.

⌒

Hang a piece of clothesline on which you can string artwork or stuffed animals.

Bathroom

Throw out expired prescription medicines and any nonprescription medicines more than two years old. They undergo changes in chemical makeup over time, causing them to lose their potency.

⌒

Antibiotics should be thrown out regardless of expiration date. They work only when taken for the prescribed course of treatment, which is usually 10 to 14 days. Taking antibiotics for less than the prescribed course builds up your body's immunity to antibiotic treatment, which can make it more difficult to treat future illnesses.

Throw out sunscreen that's more than two years old. When in doubt, throw it out, because it won't be as effective.

⁓

Keep prescription-refill labels in the medicine cabinet or wherever you keep your prescriptions. When you get down to a two-week supply, put the label in your wallet or purse, and make a note to stop at the pharmacy next time you're in that area.

⁓

Organize your medicine cabinet as you would organize any cabinet. Store like items together and store frequently used items in places that are easiest to reach.

⁓

Try to keep the sink-top free of clutter. Find a place for everything and put everything in its place.

⁓

Keep makeup in a bag or bin that can be put away in one motion instead of keeping everything loose in a drawer.

⁓

Use stacking bins or baskets to contain brushes and hair accessories.

⁓

If you have enough drawers, assign one to each household member.

Eliminate clutter in the shower and tub with caddies designed for these areas.

Store bath toys in a nylon mesh bag and hang from your tub or shower caddy.

Because the bathroom is where you use towels, that's the best place to keep them. If you have few or no shelves, consider adding a freestanding, ready-made shelving unit over the toilet. If that won't work, try using a narrow baker's rack.

If you don't have shelf space, roll towels and washcloths and store in a pretty basket near the bathtub or shower.

Install hooks, rods, or rings near the sink for hanging washcloths and hand towels.

Store hair dryers, and other hairstyling gadgets in a long wicker basket under the sink, on a shelf, or in a bathroom cupboard. Or hang hair dryers and curling irons. A simple hook inside the vanity works great.

Install a hat rack or hooks on the back of the bathroom door for hanging robes. Hang a mesh bag behind the door for dirty towels.

Under the sink, use wire baskets that stack and slide to bring cleaning products, medicines, and toiletries within easy reach.

Bedroom

Hang a nylon bag on a hook behind your bedroom door to hold items that need to go the dry cleaner. When you pick up dry-cleaned items, take them out of the plastic bags and hang them on this hook to air for one day before hanging in your closet.

~

Empty your jewelry box and lay out all your jewelry on your bed. Throw away anything that is broken beyond repair or not worth fixing. Unless you still wear them, throw away any single earrings. Put to one side the pieces that you wear often. Look at what's left and decide what you should keep; give away, sell, or donate the rest.

~

Keep earrings organized and dust-free by storing them in a clear plastic container with small compartments (like a tackle box).

~

Use ice cube trays for storing earrings — one set per cube.

~

Keep costume jewelry necklaces in a glass bowl. They look pretty and are easy to find.

The best way to keep chains from getting knotted and tangled is to hang them up. Use a stick-on plastic rod, tie rack, cup hooks, or nails.

Instead of buying another dresser, consider adding a wall system with open and closed shelving for your television, VCR, and stereo, as well as for clothing and books. They come with drawers, cabinets, and even foldout desktops.

Find a place in your room to hang some pegs that you can use for hanging your robe and for clothes that have been worn, but need airing. Or use a coat rack.

If you don't have enough height in your closet, hang long evening dresses on a hook on the back of your bedroom door.

Place pretty dishes on dresser tops and nightstands to collect loose change and other pocket paraphernalia, rings, watches, and other jewelry.

A wooden chest at the foot of the bed makes a wonderful storage place for linens, blankets, and comforters. It also makes a great place to sit when putting on or taking off your socks and shoes.

You can buy rollout drawers that attach to your bed frame for storing linens, pajamas, nightgowns, or whatever.

Bed skirts are wonderful for creating a hiding place under your bed. Store seasonal clothes or linens in clear plastic zippered bags or labeled storage bins.

Kitchen and Dining Room

What irks you about your kitchen? Take some time to think about how you can make your kitchen a more efficient and enjoyable place to work.

If the kitchen is where you handle mail and messages, consider adding a hinged countertop somewhere that can be pulled up or down as needed. Use a nearby drawer to store pens, papers, postage stamps, paper clips, rubber bands, envelopes, and note paper. Use a napkin holder for outgoing mail.

In your pantry and cupboards, have specific shelves for specific things. Label shelves so other household members can help you put away groceries.

After opening crackers, chips, cookies, or anything that comes in a bag, store them in clear plastic bins to keep them fresh and contained.

Wire racks inside cabinet doors or closet doors are terrific for storing all kinds of things.

Hang up everything you can — from pots to potholders, coffee mugs to plastic wrap.

Store things where you use them. Keep pots and pans near the stove, glasses near the refrigerator, dishes and silverware near the table. Store the box of trash bags at the bottom of your trash can.

Mount spices on a wall rack or store in a cupboard on a stepped organizer or turntable.

If you are short on space for storing spices, add a narrow shelf to the back of one cabinet.

Go through your spices and throw out any that are more than three years old. If you're not sure if they're good, open the jar and smell the contents. Pinch a small amount between two fingers and sniff. Anything? If you use certain spices infrequently, buy in smaller quantities.

Store spices alphabetically or group by category (baking, peppers, Italian) so you spend less time looking for them when you need them. Put them back with the label facing the front.

Use hanging wire mesh baskets to store fruits and vegetables. To prevent bruising, pad the bottom with a cloth napkin or tea towel.

Wire grids and S hooks are great for hanging utensils.

When replacing small appliances, consider appliances that mount under cabinets (coffeemaker, microwave, can opener). But before you go out and buy these items, ask yourself if you really need them.

Never store anything in the oven. You may remember that you put something there, but no one else will think to look first before turning on the oven.

Store gravy and seasoning packets in a narrow box that lets you flip through them to take inventory or to find the one you need.

Think of your refrigerator as a large cupboard. Designate specific shelves for specific things.

Always store leftovers in the same place in your refrigerator and check there every day to reduce the amount of food that goes to waste.

Save space in your refrigerator with under-the-shelf holders for large soda bottles.

If storage space is at a premium in your refrigerator or freezer, store leftovers in plastic food storage bags. They take up less room than plastic containers, and you won't have to find space to store all those containers when they're not being used.

If the door of your refrigerator doesn't hold all your condiments, use a square or rectangular plastic box to contain them on a shelf and use the door to store other things.

What to do with those bags you've saved? Store them near the cat litter box and use them for scooping dirty litter. Or fill an empty tissue box and then keep it in your car for use as trash bags or for carrying things into the house.

GROCERY BAG ANYONE?

To store plastic grocery bags, hang one and put all the others inside. When the bag is full, stop saving bags. Or cut a three-inch hole in the side of a plastic milk jug and stuff the bags into it. A one-gallon milk jug will hold about 100 bags. You can also recycle a large oatmeal container or coffee can to collect bags.

Add a shelf or turntable under the kitchen sink to provide easier access to kitchen cleaning items like dishwashing detergent, paper towels, and so on.

If you have unused space high in a cupboard, make use of that space by adding a freestanding wire shelf in the cupboard.

For more shelf space, add a basket or bin that hangs from a shelf.

Replace fixed shelves with adjustable shelving that rolls out. Buy a do-it-yourself kit at home or hardware stores.

If you have a wooden breadbox, nail it up under a cabinet. Make sure there are ventilation holes to prevent molding.

When deciding what goes on each shelf in your pantry, keep in mind that it takes less effort to reach up than it does to reach down. Store the things you use most at waist level or higher.

Are you using all of your pots and pans? If you can't bear to throw any out, at least divide them and set them aside. Put them in the attic or garage.

If you haven't needed them in a year, chances are you never will. Give them to someone who does need them (see "Places to Donate" in step 3).

A rolling microwave cart with shelves and a drawer is one way to create more counter space and extra storage space for cookbooks or pots and pans, and it makes everything more accessible.

Keep an extra can opener with your pet food.

Set a pretty bowl on the counter to contain keys, loose change, and pocket stuff.

Junk drawers don't have to be neat, but it helps if you can find what you know is in there. Use adjustable dividers, utility cutlery trays, or small cardboard boxes to contain similar items such as matches, candles, pens and pencils, and coupons.

Use plastic storage bags to store all kinds of small things: batteries, pens and pencils, cookie cutters, birthday candles, and candleholders.

Leave out on your counters only what you use every day. When your countertops are neat, your whole kitchen will look neat.

Get back to basics. Do you really need an electric can opener, or will a manual one do just as well?

⁓

Set your table with a tablecloth to discourage things being dumped there.

⁓

Rearrange utensils and tools so that frequently used items are handy.

⁓

Put turntables in your refrigerator. (Measure your space before you buy.)

⁓

A knife rack frees up drawer space and makes knives more accessible.

⁓

Use rubber bands to keep together sets of things like shish-kebab skewers, fondue forks, and chopsticks in drawers.

⁓

Keep your recycling bin near the kitchen trash can and ask household members to put all aluminum, glass, and plastic containers in the bin instead of the trash. If you make it convenient to recycle, it's more likely that everyone will put recyclables in the bin instead of leaving them on the counter.

Use baskets that stack and slide to provide more convenient access to pots, pans, canned goods, and dry food.

Hang pots and pans. You can buy a ceiling or wall rack, or use chains to suspend a section of a ladder from the ceiling.

Family Room and Living Room

If you and your family spend a lot of time in the family or living room — eating, watching television, reading mail, magazines, and newspapers, playing with your pets — it can go from uncluttered to cluttered in no time. You might want to think about putting a wastebasket in that room. And make sure that there's a place for everything, including remote controls and television guides, CDs, videotapes, magazines, and pet toys. Maybe you need more shelf space, but before you run out and buy shelving, see if there's anything you could give away, throw away, or sell.

Make clutter "invisible." No, this isn't a trick. But the right kind of storage can work like magic. Wire shelving tends to "disappear" into the background. And wicker baskets blend nicely with almost any decor.

End tables with drawers are handy for storing coasters, reading glasses, and playing cards. Or you can contain these items in a woven basket or pretty bowl high enough on a shelf so all you see is the basket or bowl.

If you have young children, keep a basket in the family room or living room for collecting stray toys. This is especially helpful when you have 10 minutes or less to straighten your house for last-minute visitors.

Take all your books off the shelves. Dust and put back only your favorites and pass along those books you don't wish to reread. If you didn't have your books in any particular order before, consider grouping them by category. You might keep all your novels in one section and all your nonfiction books in another, grouped by subject; for example, gardening, self-help, travel.

Unless you're using them, get rid of your college textbooks already!

Organize books by subject and alphabetize by author. If you organize books so that there is a logical place to put them back, it's less likely that they will get left out.

If you're out of space on your bookshelves, but you're not willing to part with any more books, take the largest ones off the shelves, stack them near a chair, and use the stack as an end table.

Use baskets that stack and slide to store video-tapes efficiently.

Use the space under your sofa to store game boxes, leaves from your dining room table, or for storing videotapes in bins designed for under-bed storage.

Avoid CD towers with individual, preset slots unless you don't mind searching for CDs. They look nice, but are difficult to organize. If you organize alphabetically by artist, what do you do when you buy a new CD? You have to rearrange the entire collection to make space for it.

When it comes to decorating, keep it simple. The less you have out, the less you have to keep tidy.

Home Office

If your desktop gets out of control easily, you probably have too much stuff on it that doesn't need to be there. Remove anything you don't need regular access to. You should have only what you need in front of you. Put the rest away.

Avoid piling. Use hanging files, vertical files, shelves, and backs of doors.

For home-based entrepreneurs, a well-organized office is essential. If you're working on several projects for several clients at any one time, use a small plastic cabinet with drawers. Store all the job folders for a client in one drawer, lying flat. Allow a separate drawer for each client so job folders don't get mixed up and you always know where they are when not in use. Store "dead" or inactive files in a filing cabinet or plastic storage bin.

Use a cutlery tray or drawer tray in your desk drawer to organize pens, pencils, scissors.

Set up an "in" basket and use it as a temporary holding tank for things you don't know where to put. Every month or so, go through it. The really useless stuff will have sunk to the bottom of the basket, and you can throw it out.

If you need extra working space for a big project, set up a small folding table that you can put away when you're done.

You can buy a plastic paper organizer that sits under your printer or fax and keeps stationery handy without taking up much room. Use one tray for storing recycled paper. You'll always know where to find a piece of paper to jot down a note and you'll have less paper garbage.

You can buy a monitor-top organizer with various-size slots for paper, sticky notes, rubber bands, and folders, plus holes along the back for pens, pencils, highlighters, and markers.

What's really cluttered-looking and ugly are all the cords that come out of your computer, phone, fax, modem, answering machine, etc. Get some large twist ties or plastic garbage-bag fasteners. Take a few minutes to even out all the cords and then fasten them together so they make one big rope instead of a huge snarl of wires going every which way. You can do this with your television, VCR, and stereo equipment, too.

For home-office filing systems see step 6.

Basement, Attic, and Garage

Keep in mind that items stored in your attic may be exposed to extreme temperatures. It's definitely not the place to store photographs. Basements and garages tend to be damp or wet. Be sure to store boxes off the floor on a shelf.

Construct your own inexpensive shelving out of 2×4s and ½-inch plywood. It's easy and requires no sawing. Get eight-foot 2×4s and have the lumberyard rip 4×8 sheets of plywood lengthwise to make two 2×8 pieces. Use sheetrock screws and a cordless drill to assemble. Tops can be screwed into ceiling joists for stability. Use this same arrangement to make three shelves with ten 2×4s and three sheets of plywood per shelf unit. The finished product is much stronger and cheaper than anything you can buy. And it's easier to fabricate (many purchased shelves have to be fabricated anyway).

Use deep, simple shelving that makes it easy to find boxes and allows you to sweep or vacuum underneath.

Try to keep storage boxes together along one wall.

Use plastic milk crates for storage on shelves. Give each crate a category label like "camping," "biking," "skiing," or "games." It makes things much easier to find and put away.

If you have limited storage, you might want to build or buy an outdoor storage or utility shed to contain things you use outdoors. This could include mowers and other equipment for your lawn, gardening equipment, tools and supplies, snow-removal equipment, cooking grill, and even sporting equipment such as bicycles. Don't forget to make good use of your space. What can you hang on the walls? From the ceiling? Make it work for you. And do buy a good padlock.

Before you rent storage space, carefully consider the items you are storing. Is it really worth the money to store this stuff? Or could you get rid of some or most or all of it?

If you have adult children no longer living at home, let them know that you are going to clean out the basement and ask them to come and get their stuff. If they live far away, tell them you'll keep it for six months or one year and then you are going to donate it.

Designate a large, clean trash can in the yard or garage in which children can put away outdoor toys.

Use large vinyl-covered hooks to hang up bikes, folding lawn chairs, snow shovels, snow tires, skis, and sleds.

If there's enough room in your garage, designate one wall as an indoor "parking" area for children's bicycles and riding toys. Ask children to park there whenever they're done riding.

Install hooks on beams to hang ladders horizontally.

Store bags of seed, fertilizer, pet food, salt, and sand in large plastic containers with covers to keep contents dry and to avoid spills. Label each one and keep a scoop inside each container. (Make scoops using plastic half-gallon milk containers cut diagonally across the middle.)

If you keep a wheelbarrow or cart in your garage, store it upright. It will take up less room and you won't be tempted to put anything in it, even temporarily. (Flat surfaces are like magnets for clutter.)

If you are remodeling your kitchen, save the old kitchen cabinets for instant storage in the garage or basement.

Assign one area of your garage for storage of camping, sporting, and vacation gear.

Tools, Hobbies, and Sports Equipment

Hang tools on hooks. Drill small holes near the tops of long-handled garden tools such as rakes, shovels, and pitchforks. Run a length of jute or sisal rope through the hole and knot the ends. Hang on hooks screwed into the wall.

Hang wire shelving horizontally between ceiling rafters and use S hooks for hanging tools.

For small hand tools, nail to the wall as many empty coffee cans as you need (one long nail through the top works fine).

Create storage between exposed studs. Try nailing two 2×4s horizontally across the exposed studs, one approximately one foot off the ground and the second approximately three feet off the ground. You can slide long-handled tools between the outside wall and the 2×4s. For storing shorter tools, make the boards different heights. This works for baseball bats, lacrosse and hockey sticks, and tennis rackets, too.

Recycle wooden pallets. Stand one on its side against a wall and insert long-handled tools, handles first.

Recycle cans. Cut the top and bottom from any size can and nail it to the wall with the holes facing the floor and ceiling. Place the long handles of tools through the cans.

Put an old golf bag to work as a gardening tool caddy. Use it to store rakes and shovels. Put hand tools and gloves in the pockets and you're ready for a round of gardening.

Use plastic bins of assorted sizes to store plumbing and electrical supplies.

Use chains and hooks to store tools. Hang a length of heavy-duty chain from a stud in the ceiling and place S hooks at intervals on it. Insert eye screws at the end of each tool and hang on S hooks.

HARDWARE STORAGE

Use glass jars (peanut-butter, spaghetti-sauce, or baby-food jars work great) to hold nuts and bolts, screws, nails, and miscellaneous hardware (alligator clips, odd metal fasteners, picture hangers, drapery hardware). Use a different jar for each type so you can find what you need easily.

You can also use coffee cans for storing small hardware items. Store the cans on their sides with the lid facing out and label the lid or tape a sample of what's inside to the lid. You'll just need to have something like a bookend at either end to keep the cans from rolling off the shelf.

Two nails or pegs are all you really need to hang a broom, rake, shovel, or similar gardening tools.

Make a gardening tool bucket using a large compound pail lined with a cloth insert and pockets that hang inside and outside the bucket.

Wherever possible, hang up tools and equipment leaving floor space free (a broom and dustpan holder works great).

Use pegboard with S hooks for hanging hand tools. Consider drawing a silhouette around each tool to mark its spot.

Store like items together such as friction tape, pipe thread tape, and packing tape.

A cutlery tray is useful for sorting small articles in the workbench drawer.

You can also use a plastic cutlery tray to store different size screwdrivers, wrenches, and hand tools.

Hang lumber in racks hung from the ceiling. Color-code the lengths like they do at the lumberyard; red for 10 feet, green for 12 feet, and so on.

Use clear plastic storage boxes to store opened and unopened seed packets. If you save seeds from plants, save the seed packets and you'll have a place to put them until next year.

Store paintbrushes in coffee cans, bristles up. To keep a film from developing on paint, put the lid on tight and store upside down.

Separate things into different categories: tools, paint and other household supplies, lumber, sports equipment, outdoor stuff. Section off areas for each category.

Turn one corner of your garage into a potting shed and store all your gardening and yard equipment there.

Store craft supplies in a decorative storage box, hatbox, or basket that's pretty enough to leave out in your bedroom or living room. Have one box or basket for each project so you can work on several projects at a time without creating a mess.

Old lunch boxes make portable storage boxes for all kinds of things. And they're stackable. You can peel the labels off the plastic ones and decorate them, or use them just as they are. Look for them at garage sales and thrift stores.

Use rolling storage bins with drawers for storing craft materials and supplies.

To organize sewing supplies, place like items such as buttons, spools of thread, and hooks and snaps in small plastic bags and place all the bags in a pretty covered box or decorative tin.

Plastic fishing tackle boxes are ideal for small craft supplies.

Use baskets that stack and slide for convenient access to hobby tools.

Use labeled shoe boxes for sewing and craft supplies.

A nylon hammock strung across one corner of the garage makes nifty storage for sporting equipment and keeps balls, gloves, sticks, and other gear easy to find and put away.

Rubbermaid and Lillian Vernon sell sports equipment organizers that hold all different kinds of balls, bats, gloves, and tennis rackets.

Only save the sports equipment that you and your family still uses.

Car Interiors

Get a map case for your car. Or fold maps and put them in a plastic storage bag that you keep under the passenger's seat.

⁓

If you need to keep things in the trunk that you frequently use, get as many plastic bins as you need to contain stuff by category. Put all sports equipment in one bin, camping stuff in another, beach things in another.

⁓

If you have room in the trunk, leave your cooler in the car throughout the summer months. If you decide to shop for groceries at lunchtime, you can pick up some bagged ice and keep cold items cold until you get home. The cooler gets used more often, and doesn't take up space somewhere else.

⁓

One woman describes the trunk of her car as awe-inspiring. She always has a phone book, tool-box, step-stool, a full foul-weather set (pants and windbreaker), flashlight, first-aid kit, bungee cords, spare sneakers, socks, sunscreen, and insect spray. She also keeps toys in the trunk for spontaneous playing — a kite, fishing pole, snowshoes. And why not? If you keep whatever you may need on the road in your trunk, you won't have to worry about storing it anywhere else.

Keep a plastic bag in your car for paper wrappers and other garbage. Get in the habit of emptying it whenever you fill up with gas.

When you are stopped at a traffic light, do a quick cleanup in your car. Put cassettes in cassette storage, put wrappers in the garbage bag.

Use space under the driver's seat for storing emergency items such as a flashlight, emergency road flare, and first-aid kit. Contain these items in a small plastic bin or bag.

If you listen to cassettes or CDs in your car and you don't have a cassette or CD organizer, get one.

If you really want to be organized, keep a notepad and two pens (in case one doesn't work) in your glove compartment along with your insurance and registration cards.

If you need to save receipts for gas and meals, keep an accordion-style checkbook folder under your seat so you won't lose any.

Simplify with Systems

In this chapter . . .

- *Schedules, Lists, and Notes*
- *Bills and Finances*
- *Filing Systems*
- *Mail*
- *Magazines and Newspapers*
- *Recipes and Meal Planning*
- *Getting Family Participation*
- *Laundry and Housekeeping*
- *Organizing to Go*

You've heard the saying: "Work smarter, not harder." The way to do that is to organize and simplify routine tasks with systems. That's what makes organized people so organized. Take grocery shopping, for example. Going once a week or even once every other week instead of several times a week can free up as many as two hours or more each week. Wouldn't you enjoy having an extra hour or two each week?

Another way to simplify routine tasks is to group similar tasks together. Instead of filing each piece of paper as you are finished with it, put it in a "to be filed" folder and do all your filing at one time. When you get out the iron and ironing board, iron everything that needs ironing. While you're chopping an onion for a recipe, chop extra for another night. Get it?

It also helps to create and maintain regular patterns for routine tasks. For example, get in the habit of paying bills twice a month on set dates instead of whenever the mood strikes or whenever you remember.

Create pleasant rituals out of routine tasks. In her book *Living a Beautiful Life,* Alexandra Stoddard proposes that warm, pleasant rituals help you enjoy the way you're spending your time, so you'll feel like you have more of it. And you'll no longer waste energy thinking about an unpleasant task you have to do. She suggests that you try to involve as many of the five senses as you can in creating these rituals. When it's time to pay bills, for instance, make yourself a cup of tea and put on your favorite music. Imagine looking forward to paying bills!

If mornings are hectic in your home, try to do as much as you can for the next day each night. If you have kids, get them to help you make their lunches, lay out their clothing, or set the breakfast table.

Try implementing the following systematic rules for organizing and you'll soon discover extra minutes in your day and extra hours in your week!

- Do quick little cleanups often.
- Put things away at once.
- Label everything.
- Keep frequently used items handy.
- Focus on one task at a time.
- Finish what you're doing before starting something new.
- Always look for a simpler way.
- Take care of today's things today.
- Stop procrastinating.

Schedules, Lists, and Notes

Eliminate mental clutter by making a "to do" list every morning. It frees up your brain for more important work. Write down every little task so you can enjoy crossing things off your list throughout the day.

Create a list of goals you would like to accomplish over the next one to five years. Each day, look at your master list, and add something from it to your daily "to do" list. It could be just a phone call to get information or a stop at the library to do some research. Working toward your goals every day brings you one step closer to achieving them.

Create a master list of tasks. This is the list you add to whenever you think of or discover something that needs to be done. Refer to this list every day and select those things you believe you can accomplish that day. Keep in mind that just about everything takes longer than you think.

Group errands together geographically. If you're going to the bank, look at your master list of things to do and see if there's another stop or two you could make in that area. Consolidating your driving time can free up time for doing other, more enjoyable things.

Create a tickler file. It's simple, inexpensive, and reduces paper clutter like you wouldn't believe. Make one folder for each month of the year and one file for each day of the month (1–31). Use the monthly folders to file things you will need in the coming months. Use the day of the month files to keep track of things you need this month on a particular date. You can file bills to be paid, notes about promises you made or promises made to you, birthday cards, directions to an upcoming party, airplane tickets, and whatever else you might need for a future date. Each day, take out what is in today's folder and then place the empty folder at the back of the numbered folders. At the end of each month, put the next month's items into the day-of-the-month folders.

Write all anniversaries and birthdays on a yearly calendar. At the end of the year, transfer those dates to your new calendar. That way you'll never forget a special occasion.

~

Instead of shopping for cards one at a time, buy all the cards you'll need for several months or a whole year and file them in your tickler file. Lightly pencil the recipient's name on the envelope, or go ahead and address and stamp them now to save time later.

~

Some people prefer to use a 3×5 card file to keep track of things to do. Use dividers with labels to create your own categories such as "today," "to buy," and "goals."

~

Do you need a planner? That's up to you. Should you use a daily, weekly, or monthly planner? If you need to write a lot in your planner each day, you might need a daily planner. If you need to see a week at a glance, a weekly planner will be better for you. Most daily and weekly planners also have a monthly planning guide that lets you see the month at a glance.

~

When you write appointments in your planner, also write in directions and a phone number to call in case you're running late or need to reschedule.

If it seems like you can never find time to do a particular thing, schedule an appointment with yourself to do it. While you're at it, schedule a half-hour of uncluttering time each day!

Whether you use a planner or not, eliminate having notes all over by keeping a spiral bound, pocket-size notebook with you at all times. Start each day by putting the date on the top of the page and write your "to do" list on that page. Throughout the day, jot down anything you need to remember: people's names, ideas, notes from telephone conversations. Start a new page each day. Clip a pen to the spiral binding, so you're never without one.

Don't leave things out as a reminder to do something with them. Put the item where it belongs, jot yourself a note, and put the note in your tickler file.

What about notes to other family members? Get a magnetic message board for your refrigerator. Train everyone to record and look for messages there.

A message center is a must in a busy household. Designate one area where mail and telephone messages are left for other family members. Keep a notepad and pen near the telephone. Make it the responsibility of the message taker to leave the message in the designated area.

For keeping track of family members' where-abouts, get a doctor's scheduling calendar that lets you see where everyone is (or needs to be) at a particular time. Attach the calendar to the refrigerator with a large magnetic clip.

Another way to manage family schedules is with a dry-erase board with a pocket for colored markers and an eraser, and a cork strip for pinning up miscellaneous items. Use a black marker to make a column down the left side of the board and write in the days of the week. Make a column across the top of the board and write in each family member's name, using a different color marker for each one. Before the start of each week, write in the dates for the days of the week. Then, using the appropriate color marker for each individual, write in appointments, meetings, practices, games, and family celebrations and outings.

For keeping track of important due dates for schoolchildren, permission slips, or supplies needed on a particular day, read and highlight notes from school, arrange in order of date, and post them on the refrigerator with a large magnetic clip. Or file them in your tickler file.

Create checklists for things you need to remember on a regular basis, such as instructions for the baby-sitter or pet-sitter.

If you take the time to master the technology, scheduling software can be used alone or with a companion notebook organizer. Some programs will even notify you of upcoming events or due dates. You can use scheduling software to help you manage family schedules as well as your own time. And you can try it for free. To download a free trial copy of Time and Chaos, a personal information management program, go to http://www.isbister.com. To try any one of a number of Day-Timer scheduling programs, go to http://www.daytimer.com/technology/software/download/soft1.html.

If you think of something while at work that you need to do when you get home, call your answering machine and leave yourself a message to jog your memory. It eliminates notes and somehow gives the item a higher priority for getting done.

Bills and Finances

Throughout the month, keep charge-card receipts and bank deposit and withdrawal slips in a folder or envelope labeled "Monthly Receipts." Use these receipts to double-check the accuracy of your statement and then toss them.

When you receive bills in the mail, save only the bill and the return envelope and throw everything else away. This eliminates about half of the paper volume. Place the bill in the envelope. Fold the envelope flap backward against the front of the envelope, write the amount due and due date on it and file it in your tickler file. On bill-paying day, write the check, enter it into your checkbook register or ledger, mail the bill, and file the receipt.

Pay bills twice a month. Use a folder with two pockets — one for bills to be paid on the first of the month and one for bills to be paid on the fifteenth.

FINANCIAL SOFTWARE

If you're fairly organized and willing to spend some time mastering the technology, financial software packages can help minimize paper mess and save you hours each month. Programs like Quicken are useful for managing your checkbook (no more math errors and bounced checks!) and keeping track of investments. For an extra fee each month, you can use Quicken to pay your bills electronically so you have no checks to write, and need no envelopes or stamps! You can even "ask" simple questions like "How much did I spend on groceries this year?" The answers will help you develop a more accurate budget based on actual spending.

Keep this folder handy so that you can put bills into the appropriate pocket when they arrive.

~

Another way to manage bills is to put all unpaid bills in one folder with a list of each bill and the amount due in order of due date. As you pay each bill, cross it off the list. Add new bills to the bottom of the list. Write check numbers on paid bills and file in folders designated for each specific category; e.g., telephone, cable, car insurance.

~

An alternative method is to fill a three-ring binder with pocket folders for filing receipts by category. You can keep track of payments by writing the check number, amount, and date paid on each folder. This method is handy if you have a lot of household expenses that are tax deductible, because you've got everything in one place come tax time. And it eliminates filing monthly bills.

~

Address a batch of envelopes for paying those monthly bills that do not include reply envelopes such as rent payments and coupon book loans. You might as well place a postage stamp and return address label on them while you're at it.

~

Keep track of when bills are due by writing due dates on a yearly calendar that lets you see one month at a glance. Note paydays on the calendar as well.

Use automated payment services. If you have a credit card or loan through your bank or credit union, you may be able to transfer funds from your checking or savings account using a touch-tone telephone. Many utility companies also offer this service which ensures that the bill is paid on time and eliminates both the need to write checks and the expense of mailing them each month.

Have your bank keep your checks. If you need to find a canceled check (and how often do you really need to do that?), simply request it. Some banks are actually charging customers to continue receiving canceled checks with monthly statements.

If you work from home, file receipts by category: utilities, office supplies, advertising, postage. Keep all receipts in 8×10 envelopes by category. Pay all your bills by check and save your bank statements. Use a spiral-bound notebook to keep track of tax-deductible travel, entertainment, and meals. Include a note of the time, date and place, and the nature of the business conducted. For expenditures over $25, you'll also need the receipt.

Filing Systems

Set up a filing system. Whatever filing system you use should make it easy to find what you need, be easy to maintain, and make sense to everyone who needs to use it.

File only what you really need to file. On average, 80 percent of what is filed is never looked at again. So if you spend a total of one hour each month filing, you are wasting 48 minutes every month.

If you don't have a den or office, keep a rolling file cabinet in a closet.

Before you start filing, go through your piles and throw out anything with an expiration date, anything that no longer interests you, and anything that has been sitting in that pile for more than a year, unless you need it for your taxes. (Refer to "Retaining Records" box in this chapter for a guide to what you can safely toss.)

File daily, weekly, monthly, or quarterly depending on the volume of paper.

If you don't file regularly, at least put all items to be filed in a "to be filed" folder or basket.

Keep all tax documentation in one place so that it's handy when you're ready to prepare your taxes.

The easiest system is to file by subject: bills, credit cards, insurances, loans, receipts, etc.; and within these categories, file alphabetically.

Color-code folders. Color-coding makes it easier to identify which files are which without even reading the file name, and makes finding the appropriate files a split-second task. It also looks nice, which makes filing more pleasant.

If you color-code files, keep your coding system simple. Limit the number of colors you use to four or five. Use different colored file folders for different categories. For example, you could use green for money files (bills, receipts, investments), yellow for insurance policies, blue for warranties, red for copies of important documents (wills, birth and marriage certificates), and orange for filing fun stuff like day-trip ideas or articles on gardening or crafts.

Keep filing in perspective. When giving a name to a new file, think of what heading you are likely to look for the next time you need the file. Don't think too long about this. The first thing that springs to mind is probably the best file name.

Start file names with a noun (person, place, or thing). A single noun is usually all you need.

Sort all things to be filed into 15 to 20 basic categories. You can always combine or eliminate categories later. Set aside anything you're having difficulty categorizing.

THE SHOE-BOX METHOD

Another method for filing is what's known as the shoe-box method, a numeric filing system. Put all papers to be filed in one large cardboard box. Pick up the first paper. Is it outdated? Toss it. If it's something you want to file like a receipt for an item with a warranty, label your first hanging folder with the number one. Write "I — Receipts and Warranties" on the receipt and file it in a folder marked "I — Receipts and Warranties." Now start a master list that begins with "I — Receipts and Warranties." Repeat the process with the next piece of paper, a new hanging file and file folder, and note the addition on your master list. Keep going until everything is filed. When you are looking for something, find the category on the list and go to the hanging file with the corresponding number. You can put as many subjects as you wish in one hanging file. Keep your master list in a hanging file labeled with the number zero. Keep all your papers in the box until you have time to file; if you're looking for something recent, you know where to find it.

To keep the number of files in your system to a minimum, use broad headings that will allow room for several subcategories. For example, use "insurance" as the name for one hanging file, and within it keep folders for car insurance, house insurance, and life insurance.

In addition to files for standard household categories such as bank, credit cards, insurance, and warranties, you may want to create files for job-related information, membership information, pets, or hobbies.

Once everything is filed, file regularly. Meanwhile, tackle your filing one stack at a time or for 10 to 15 minutes each day until it's all done.

INDEXING SOFTWARE

If you have a home office and find that you waste a lot of time searching for documents, Kiplinger's Taming The Paper Tiger software may be the solution. The Paper Tiger combines an easy-to-use computer indexing system with the proven paper-management methods of one of the nation's leading authorities on organizing, Barbara Hemphill. This Windows-based software lets you file and search for documents using any number of key words for quick retrieval. It cuts organizing time in half. And it comes with a unique 60-day guarantee: "Find any document in your office within five seconds . . . or your money back." Using this system, you can also index recipes, items in storage, or anything else in your home. For more information or to order, visit The Paper Tiger Web site at http://www.thepapertiger.com.

Create "hot files" for those files you access frequently. Make space in a handy filing cabinet or desk drawer (within arm's reach) or use a freestanding bin into which you can put hanging folders.

Label all file folders. If you wish, write the name of the folder at the top of each document within the folder so you know exactly where it belongs when it's time to refile it.

Avoid labeling files and folders as "miscellaneous." It's either important enough to have its own label or not important enough to save.

Align hanging file tabs on the front of the folder so that they can be seen even when the folder is full.

Once your filing system is in place, align hanging file tabs in a zigzag pattern. Use the slot on the far left and then the far right and repeat so you have just two columns of tabs showing and all tabs can be seen easily.

Always put new documents in the front of the folder, so your files are in reverse chronological order.

Once a year, go through your folders and throw away anything that's obsolete.

Retaining Records

Most of us save more paperwork than is necessary, and we do it because we think we have to or because we've always saved everything. But really, how often do you refer back to your cable bill? Or your credit-card statements? If your answer is "never," then filing these things is a waste of time and energy, not to mention a waste of filing space.

Following is a guide to what you should save and what you can toss quite safely.

Paycheck stubs. Check each one for accuracy and toss. If you are planning to apply for a loan before you next payday, save the most recent stub as proof of income.

Deposit slips. Verify them on your bank statement and then toss.

Bank statements and canceled checks. Save bank statements and canceled checks for one year, or three full tax years if you itemize expenses on your tax return.

Credit-card statements. Check to be sure that your account was credited for the correct amount and that all new charges are correctly billed. Toss last month's bill and keep the new one until the next statement is received.

Utility bills. When the next bill arrives, check to make sure your account was credited for the correct amount and toss the old bill.

Tax returns. Keep tax returns for six full tax years. Keep records of income and expenses for three tax years. That's how long the IRS has to audit your return. All tax deductions must be backed up by receipts and canceled checks. If your bank keeps your canceled checks and you are audited, you can request the ones you need for a nominal fee. If you underreport your income by 25 percent or more, the IRS has six years to audit your return. And if you don't file returns at all, the IRS can audit at any time. Store tax returns and all receipts in large manila envelopes. Label each envelope "Tax Return 19XX." File it away in a remote corner. You'll only need it again if you get audited. If you wish, you can destroy tax returns that are older than six tax years. It's best to shred or burn them because of the ease with which your identity can be stolen.

Insurance policies and bills. Save insurance policies for the period in which they are in effect. Save each monthly bill until the next one is received to check that your account was properly credited. Toss canceled insurance policies and related statements.

Receipts. If you use a credit or debit card to make purchases, save all receipts from these purchases to verify the amounts on your statement and then toss them. Actually, it's not a bad idea to save all merchandise

continued on page 136

receipts for 30 days. If you discover that the item is defective or it's the wrong size or color, you can return it for a refund or exchange it with a receipt. If an item comes with a warranty, save the receipt with the warranty. It's a good idea to save receipts for expensive articles of clothing so that you have documentation of the value in the event that an item gets lost or ruined by the dry cleaner. You may want to save receipts for furniture and other large-ticket items (say, anything over $100) in a safe-deposit box, along with photos and a household inventory to document replacement value. Toss all receipts for items you no longer own.

Legal documents. Use a safe-deposit box or fireproof lockbox to store the following documents: mortgages; marriage, death, and birth certificates; leases; trust papers; bonds.

File in a loose-leaf binder only when you need to keep similar topics together for reference or need to bring that information with you for meetings.

If you want to keep a binder in your filing cabinet with related items, look for hanging binders in your office-supply store. They're especially handy for storing newsletters, phone lists, or manuals.

Do not store your will in a safe-deposit box because the box will be sealed upon your death. Have your attorney keep the original and file a copy at home.

Real-estate records. Keep mortgage records for as long as you own your home. Keep records of real-estate improvements and the cost of selling your property even after you've sold it. This includes expenses on rental properties and second homes.

Investment records. Keep all investment records and bank statements related to investments. It is not necessary to keep the prospectus from year to year.

Other. If you have had a history of bad credit, or if your bank or credit company has made mistakes on your billing, keep those bills, along with any correspondence you have sent or received.

Set up a file for each child to include social security numbers, medical forms, school transcripts, and report cards.

Once you get your filing system and the rest of your house in order, make a home inventory list and take photographs of each room. Store in a safe-deposit box or fireproof lockbox.

File operating manuals and warranties in file folders and file alphabetically by appliance. Keep the receipt with the documentation. This will make it significantly easier to follow up with the store or company if there is a warranty problem. Keep the warranties, manuals, and receipts for as long as you own the item. Such documents can also be organized in a large three-ring binder with clear plastic pockets. Divide pockets with tabs labeled A to Z.

Mail

Open mail daily. Don't let it pile up.

~

Open mail near the garbage can. If it's garbage, throw it out immediately. It's up to you whether you want to open it first and decide, or use clues on the envelope to help you make your decision. *Hint:* If it's important, it will have first-class postage or a first-class, presorted indicia.

~

Sort mail and put everything where it belongs. Put all bills in your bill-keeping place (see "Handling Bills and Finances" in this chapter). Put things to read where you do your reading. If something requires action, put it in your tickler file (see "Schedules, Lists, and Notes" in this chapter). Divide mail for other household members or leave it all in a basket for them to sort through.

Unsolicited Mail

To reduce the amount of unsolicited mail you receive, send a postcard or letter to the Direct Marketing Association, asking to have your name removed from all lists. Be sure to include your name and address exactly as it appears on the mail you receive. If you are receiving mail to two or more different names or addresses, include this information as well, exactly as it appears on the mailings. You can tape sample mailing labels to your postcard or letter if that's easier for you. Send to: Mail Preference Service, P.O. Box 9008, Farmington, NY 11735-9008.

Another source of unsolicited mail is the credit bureau. Call the three major credit reporting agencies at the numbers listed below to request that they remove your name from the lists, which they make available to credit-card companies and some direct marketers. Your name will be removed for two years or permanently, if you request it.

- Equifax, 800–556–4711
- Experian, 800–353–0809
- Trans–Union, 800–680–7293

If you are receiving duplicate copies of catalogs, send both labels to the cataloger with one label crossed out. You'll have less mail to handle and you'll be doing your part to save trees!

Don't feel you have to look at every catalog that comes in the door. If you have favorites, limit yourself to one at a time. When the new one arrives, throw out the old one. If you see something you might like to buy in the near future, tear out the page along with the order form and back cover (the order-takers always ask for the source code on the back of your catalog). Put these pages in your tickler file. Throw out the rest of the catalog.

Handling each piece of mail only once is a good rule of thumb, but that doesn't mean sitting down right away to respond to a letter. Your friend might appreciate the quick response, but it may not be the most effective use of your time. Put the letter in a folder in your letter-writing place and make a note in your master to-do list. Taking action is more important than handling mail only once, and it's far better than putting something in a pile.

Use a Rolodex for your personal phone/address directory. If an address or phone number changes, simply fill out a new card and throw out the old one. You'll never have to update an entire address book again! If you're going on vacation and want to take some addresses with you to send postcards, pull those cards, keep them in alphabetical order, secure them with a rubber band, and put them in a small plastic bag (just in case!). Then refile them when you get home.

An alternative to the Rolodex is to use 3×5 cards stored in a pretty recipe box. On the back of the card, include wedding anniversaries and birth dates. In some cases, you may wish to record clothing sizes or color preferences so you can take the card with you when shopping for gifts.

Attach a tiny sticky tab to the cards you search for most frequently.

Whatever method you use for storing phone numbers and addresses, be sure to include E-mail addresses. You might have them in your computer, but by also writing them in your personal directory, you'll have a backup. E-mail, by the way, not only makes it easy to keep in touch, it also saves money and eliminates paper mess.

When you receive mail from someone, check the return address against the one you have in your personal address/phone directory to make sure you've got the most current address.

Magazines and Newspapers

Don't feel that you absolutely must catch up on back issues. Where is it written that you must? If you missed a few issues, just pick up your reading with the most recent issue.

Cancel any subscriptions to magazines you aren't reading. If you have not yet read the last three issues, ask yourself why. Maybe you're just not interested in it anymore. Did you know you can get a refund for the unused portion of your subscription?

～

If you're having trouble keeping up with your reading, but you don't want to cancel a subscription, set aside a regular reading time. Try turning off the television at 9:00 P.M. or not turning it on until then.

～

Keep articles you wish to read in your briefcase for something to do when you're waiting at the doctor's, commuting, or traveling on business.

～

Keep the latest issue and recycle or donate the rest. Take magazines to a nearby hospital, nursing home, gym, hospice, or wherever people spend time waiting.

～

A very busy executive might scan the table of contents of selected magazines, check off the articles that appeal to her, and then ask her assistant to clip those articles and put them in her briefcase. Then she can read them when she has downtime. You can do the same for yourself. Clip the articles you wish to save and throw away the magazine. Then put the articles in a basket or box near your favorite chair or at your bedside where you can read at your leisure. Instead of a pile that's a foot tall, you have a stack that's no more than a few inches.

Recipes and Meal Planning

If you are not currently planning meals, start now. Planning and shopping for a week's worth of meals at once takes far less time and effort than doing it each night. It ensures that you'll have everything you need in your refrigerator and cupboards, thereby eliminating extra trips to the store. You may also find that you eat healthier when you plan your meals.

When you plan weekly meals, plan to double one meal and freeze half for another night when you will be too busy to cook or just want a break. For best taste, use within one month of freezing.

Make meal planning a less time-consuming task. Use an extra calendar or index cards to keep track of what you make for dinner each night for a month and, if necessary, the location of the recipe; e.g., Betty Crocker, p. 121. When you're ready to do your weekly grocery shopping, select seven meals from your list and then refer to the recipes for the ingredients you need to add to your shopping list.

Post your weekly meal plan on the refrigerator as a reminder to defrost meat or prepare food in advance.

Organize your shopping list by aisle in your favorite supermarket. The next time you are at the market, as you go up and down the aisles, make a note of the aisle number and what items can be found in that aisle. Be sure to include the items you buy most frequently and leave off the items you never buy. Then write or type up a form that allows you to circle, cross off, or write in items you need.

FREE GROCERY LIST FORM

For a free grocery list form, go to http://freeweb. pdq.net/bman/grocery.htm.

Develop a grocery list form that includes the items you buy on a regular basis (milk, cheese, bread, eggs, butter, flour) plus blank lines for other items. Make 10 copies of the form and attach them to the side of the refrigerator with a large magnetic clip. Keep a magnetic pen handy. When you run out of something, make a check mark near the item or use the blank lines to write it on the list immediately. It greatly reduces the chance of not having something you need when you need it. It also reduces trips to the supermarket. Get your whole family in the habit of using the grocery form.

Do you save coupons? Do you use them? Do you really save money using them? While saving coupons can save money, it also takes time to clip, file, retrieve, and use coupons. If you weigh the cost of your time against the savings, you may find that your time could be better spent elsewhere. You might even be able to save just as much money or more by comparing unit prices.

If you do use coupons, store them in an accordion-style canceled check file, recipe box, or lunch box with index tabs.

If you organize your shopping list by aisle, organize your coupons the same way. Use aisle numbers as divider tabs in your coupon organizer or label individual envelopes with the aisle numbers.

Take out the coupons you plan to use each week and put them in an old checkbook case along with your list and a pen to cross off items as you shop. It's also helpful if you mark with a "C" the items on your list for which you have coupons.

Write your shopping list on the back of a used envelope and put your coupons inside it.

Bring a clothespin to the supermarket. As you find the coupon items, clip those coupons to your shopping cart.

If you like to clip recipes out of magazines, file them in file folders by category or in a large envelope labeled "Recipes." When you're looking for something different to make for dinner, go through your file and select a recipe. If it's good, add it to your permanent collection. If you didn't care for it, simply discard it.

Create your own recipe book using a three-ring photo album with magnetic pages. The plastic pages keep your recipes clean and allow you to store recipes from any number of sources and in any number of formats, from index cards to magazine clippings to laser-printed recipes. The three-ring format allows you to add divider tabs and pocket folders for storing recipes you have not yet tried. You can start by creating one book

DOWNLOAD RECIPES

Instead of buying cookbooks or cooking magazines, download or print recipes from the Internet and create your own cookbook of favorites. You'll find more than 36,000 recipes including many ethnic recipes at http://soar.berkeley.edu/recipes/. At this Web site, you can search for recipes by ingredients, which is very handy if you happen to have a surplus of vegetables or herbs from your garden or if you're tired of preparing chicken the same old ways.

Another good source that also includes links to other Web sites with recipes is the Internet Chef at http://www.ichef.com/ichef-recipes/.

For a wide variety of information, ranging from Thanksgiving recipes to a cook's thesaurus of substitutions and nutritional information on fast foods, check out http://www.mel.lib.mi.us/reference/REF-food.html.

If you want fat-free recipes for bread, salads, casseroles, ethnic foods, and more, check out http://www.fatfree.com and if you've got a craving for cookies, you'll find more than 1,300 cookie recipes at http://www.cookierecipe.com.

of your favorite recipes. Eventually, you might like to create several books for different types of recipes such as entertaining, holiday, desserts, or family recipes.

Getting Family Participation

Set expectations. Have a family meeting and lay down the rules. Establish Rule #1: Whoever makes a mess is responsible for cleaning it up — now, not later. That means every household member is responsible for cleaning up his or her own bathroom mess, kitchen mess, and bedroom mess. It also means putting away outside stuff including bicycles, balls, tools, soda cans, and other trash.

Establish other house rules:

- If you take it out, put it back.
- If you borrow it, return it.
- If you open it, close it.
- If you drop it, pick it up.
- If you take if off, hang it up.
- If you break it, fix it.

Make chores a family project. Have some fun doing it together. Tackle each room together. No one leaves the room until it's done.

Explain how you are trying to unclutter the house so you can have more time to spend with them. Ask them what they can do to help and write down their suggestions. Let your family know how much their support means to you.

Play clutter tag. To make other family members more aware of their clutter trails, get a roll of stickers (any kind will do) and for one week tag each item that's left out. Just making them aware may make them think twice about leaving things out. Children may enjoy helping you tag items, and the act of tagging will make them more likely to put away their own belongings.

If family members leave their things where they don't belong, gather them up in a large garbage bag and take it out to the garage. When they ask if you've seen a particular item you picked up, tell them it's in the garage. When they ask why, tell them you found it lying around and thought it was garbage. They should get the idea pretty fast.

Make it clear that leaving personal belongings unattended may result in their being held for ransom. If a family member wants his or her stuff back, he or she will have to do an extra chore. If anyone chooses not to do the chore, you know that the item isn't important to him or her. Give the item away or throw it away without guilt.

Establish playtime rules. Teach very young children to take out only a few toys at a time. If they've already got two or three toys out, they must put one away.

If you save coupons, have children help you go through them and throw out the expired ones. If you take them shopping with you, have them locate the coupon item for you. Some parents offer children cash for the value of the coupons in return for helping to do the shopping, loading and unloading the car, and putting food away.

Picking up is even more boring for children than it is for adults. Get creative. Make it fun for children to help.

Make helping time a time when you can spend quality, one-on-one time with your children. You might, for example, have children take turns helping to prepare dinner. During this time together, you can ask your child about school projects, talk about upcoming plans, and have some fun. Don't be surprised when your children start looking forward to their turn.

Praise children for their accomplishments to reinforce the learning of organization skills — skills that will help them throughout their lives.

Rotate jobs everyone hates. Create a job wheel with chores on the outside and names on the inside.

Help children learn to prioritize. Let them know that organizing clothes and other belongings is more important than organizing a CD collection. Help them see, too, that doing their homework is more important than straightening their rooms, but that they must finish both before getting permission to go to a friend's house for the night.

If necessary, restrict your kids' toys to one room of the house.

Create a job jar for jobs that fall outside the weekly routine. Assign a "salary" to each job.

Tell kids that whatever you find lying on the floor at a certain time will go into the garbage. Then do it. Throw out or donate the first thing that gets left out. A variation of this that works very well for younger children is to tell them that whatever the vacuum cleaner touches either gets vacuumed up or goes in the garbage. Once they see that you mean business, they'll scramble to pick up their things when you get out the vacuum cleaner.

If you tried one approach and it didn't work, try a different approach.

Give a specific time frame for chores. Daily morning expectations for all children should include:

- Make beds.
- Put away clean clothes.
- Put dirty clothes in hampers.
- Clean up bathroom mess.

⁓

Get your family to participate in a household purge twice a year. Just before Christmas and at least once more during the year, ask kids for donations of toys, books, and clothes they no longer use or want. Help them feel good about sharing their wealth by giving these things to kids who don't have any.

⁓

With older children and teenagers, make it clear that privileges depend on response to family requests. If assigned chores don't get done on time, no privileges are awarded. Privileges include going to a friend's house after school or overnight, going to the movies or roller-skating, or other extracurricular activities.

⁓

Let your children take turns being boss for 10 minutes. Their job is to supervise the other children as they pick up their belongings and straighten up their rooms. In learning to be a good supervisor, children also learn to pay more attention to details.

If picking up toys is an issue in your home, try this approach. When it's time to pick up toys, tell kids that they can't do anything else until their toys are picked up. Just state the fact and don't make a big issue out of it. If you get flak, don't argue with them, just go about your business. When they want to do something, which won't be long, tell them they can have it or do it just as soon as they put away their toys. Be firm.

Recognize that when you make dramatic changes in your life, it takes time for loved ones to accept those changes. If, for example, you have always been the messy one in the house, it's possible that family members have been using your messiness as an excuse to be messy themselves. Be patient. Eventually they will see that the old excuses no longer work.

Kids want their privacy. Let them know that if they keep their rooms picked up, you will not have to enter except for occasional, pre-announced inspections.

Assign a "put away" basket or bin to each child with his or her name on it. It's easier to carry a basket full of things than it is to carry individual items, so you might get fewer complaints when it's time to pick up. Plus, if you find anything throughout the day, you can just throw it in the appropriate box and let that kid put it away.

Picking up is more fun for young children if you give them a pillowcase.

⌒

Make it a game for kids to straighten up their rooms before bedtime. Use a stopwatch or timer and have them race against time or each other. Reward their efforts by giving them a snack or reading a book to them.

⌒

Establish a "penalty box." If mom or dad has to pick up something one of the kids left out, it will be forfeited until Saturday morning. To reclaim the item, its owner must pay a penalty of one extra chore.

CYBER MOMS

If you would like to chat on-line with other moms about organizing ideas (or parenting ideas), visit Moms Online at http://www. momsonline.com. This information-packed Web site features a chat room and a message board where you can post questions. Another excellent (and award-winning) site for information is The Dollar Stretcher at http://www. stretcher.com where you can search for articles by topic.

Blow the whistle on clutter. Every once in a while, blow a whistle and involve the whole family in a quick game of "Five-Minute Pick Me Up." The object of the game is to see who can pick up the most stuff in five minutes. Reward the winner with a couple of quarters or allow him or her to stay up a few minutes later that night.

Help kids see the relationship between clutter (or lack of clutter) and time. On a day or evening when the house is tidy, let kids know that because there's no clutter to pick up, you have time to make popcorn or cookies or whatever they're always asking for.

Set a timer each night for a 15-minute family pickup time. Use a timer that you can hear ticking. Start in the room that needs the most picking up. When it looks good to you, yell, "Kitchen!" or "Bathroom!" and move on. At the end of the 15 minutes, give each other a hug and say goodnight.

Assign a point value to tasks and have kids keep track of their points. Assign a reward for various point levels. For example, 25 points might earn the chance to stay up one-half hour later on a weekend night.

Have a garage sale and let the kids keep the money they get for selling their toys.

If you have a child who likes to save everything, give him or her a box in which to save these wonderful treasures. Everything else should be put in its place — clothes in the closet and dresser drawers; games, toys, and books where they belong. Once a week, help your child go through the box. If he or she wants to keep an item, help find a place for it. If there's no room for it, it must be discarded or another item already outside the box has to be thrown out or donated.

Laundry and Housekeeping

Try to incorporate laundry and weekly chores into your weekdays, so you don't have to spend time on the weekend doing them. And you'll be free to play!

Laundry is quicker and easier to do when clothes are already separated; you can tell at a glance when it's time to throw in a load. A very effective method is to have a white basket for white clothes, a light-colored basket for light colors, and a dark basket for dark colors. Or invest in a double or triple clothes hamper that encourages family members to separate dirty clothes. You can find these mesh hampers with plastic frames at many mass merchandisers and bed and bath stores.

To avoid losing baby socks, pin to a larger article of clothing and then wash and dry.

For very young children, make a game of tossing laundry into hampers. Give one kiss for each item that makes it in without assistance.

If you really dislike matching socks, train everyone in the household to pin socks together. Or put all the clean socks in a basket and have children sort them while you sort everything else. Not only does it teach the value of teamwork, it's also a way to spend some time together getting things done. For younger children, make a game out of sock matching. The winner is the one who has the most pairs of socks when there are no more socks left in the basket.

Assign a laundry basket to each household member. Use different colors or write their names on a piece of masking tape. Make it the responsibility of each household member to check the laundry room each day, bring their clothes to their rooms, and return the basket. Or make it a rotating chore. One day, one member distributes the laundry and returns the baskets and the next day, it's someone else's job.

If you have shelves (or room to add shelves), store clean and folded laundry on the shelves. Assign one shelf for each household member and make it their responsibility to come and get it. If anyone leaves something for more than two weeks, that person has too many clothes. Help him or her pare down.

Color-code your children's clothing. Dot clothing tags and the toes of socks using a different colored laundry marker for each child.

⁓

Eliminate the ironing basket. Remove clothes from the dryer and hang them up as soon as possible to avoid wrinkles. Take care of ironing right away or hang up unironed clothes in your closet. When you need to iron something, iron as many items as you have time for.

⁓

Start a load of wash in the morning and throw it in the dryer when you return home. Do not leave your dryer running when you leave home.

⁓

Teach your family to turn shirts, pants, and socks right side out so you don't have to do it for everyone in the house.

⁓

Develop a schedule for a laundry and let everyone know that anything that needs to be washed should be in the laundry room by 8:00 A.M. and can be picked up after 8:00 P.M.

⁓

Make sure you aren't washing towels unnecessarily. Assign a towel set to each household member to use for one week. Make sure they hang up towels after they use them.

If you don't have enough room in your laundry, keep a folding table handy or sort and fold laundry on your bed. Having enough room makes this chore faster and easier.

Make your bed every day. It doesn't have to be perfect. If you share a bed, make it a rule that the last one up makes the bed. Get up earlier every day and you may never have to make the bed again!

Using a comforter instead of a bedspread makes it easier to make the bed.

When it's time to change sheets, take them off, wash them, and put them right back on the bed. It eliminates having to fold them, put them away, and get them out again at a later date. Switch to a different set when the seasons change.

Store extra soap, shampoo, and toilet paper in the bathroom.

Store cleaning supplies where you use them. Having everything you need close at hand makes it easy to do quick little cleanups. Under your bathroom sink, keep a sponge, tub and tile cleaner, toilet cleaner and brush, a roll of paper towels, and glass cleaner. Hide a can of furniture polish and a rag somewhere in your living room.

*Excellence is doing ordinary things
extraordinarily well.*

— John W. Gardner

Instead of cleaning the whole house at once, clean one room or do one chore like dusting or vacuuming each day.

Wear an apron with a pocket while cleaning so you can carry around cleaning supplies.

Doing all the housework yourself is not doing your children any favors. Get your children to help with laundry, dishes, cleaning, and other chores. Offer a per-job salary or weekly allowance as incentive. Inspecting each chore as it's done and giving praise helps build self-esteem.

Do a little at a time, more often. If you spend five minutes cleaning the bathroom, three times a week, it takes only fifteen minutes total. But if you wait to do it once a week, it can take a half hour to cut through the buildup of clutter and dirt.

Time the tasks you hate doing. If you find that they only take five minutes, you might not mind doing them so much.

Trade the task you most hate doing with another household member's most hated task.

Organizing to Go

Prepack your favorite overnight bag or suitcase with standard travel items like an alarm clock and travel-size toiletries.

～

If you travel often, consider keeping your cosmetics in a hang-up cosmetic bag with clear plastic pouches. When it's time to pack, simply wrap it to go!

～

Before you pack for a trip, make a list of what you will need so you don't forget anything when you're packing. Take along the list in your suitcase so you make sure you don't leave anything behind when you return. While away, if you think of something you wish you had brought, add it to your packing list for next time and keep the list in your suitcase.

～

Use small, clear bags in your handbag to organize similar items like cosmetics. You'll find it's much easier to find things and easier to transfer the contents to different handbags.

Film canisters come in handy as travel aids. Use them as pillboxes for daily vitamins and other pills. Or fill canisters with small quantities of hand cream, shampoo, or conditioner. Moisten cotton balls with perfume and store in a film canister, or use canisters for earrings and rings. To make a travel sewing kit, wrap black thread around one end of two toothpicks and white thread around the other end. Place in canister with a sewing needle, safety pins, and a couple of buttons.

＊

If you don't have a pocket in your handbag for your keys, pin a large safety pin to the lining and get in the habit of pinning your keys there.

＊

Prepack your gym bag with a list of what you need to take with you; for example, sneakers, socks, shorts and shirt, headband, water bottle, toiletries, and towel. You'll be amazed at how much easier it will be to pack the bag each time you need it. And you'll never end up at the gym without your sneakers or a towel for your shower!

＊

Prepack other bags, too, like beach bags and kids' overnight bags so that you can be ready to go quickly. If your kids play several different sports, consider having one bag for each sport.

To make outdoor entertaining easier, keep a storage bin near the back door that contains paper plates, plastic glasses and tableware, a tablecloth, barbecue utensils, citronella candles, and bug repellent.

~

Consider keeping separate briefcases for separate work. This is very helpful if you are active on various committees and boards. Prepacking your briefcase saves valuable time and ensures that you always have what you need for meetings.

Ban Clutter Forever

In this chapter . . .

- *Paper Clutter*
- *Gift Getting*
- *Kick the Shopping Habit*
- *Daily Rituals*
- *Periodic Purges*
- *Final Thoughts*

Getting organized is simple. Staying organized takes discipline, but you will love the freedom from stress and the freedom to spend more time doing what you enjoy.

There are three simple rules for maintaining a clutter-free home:

Rule #1: For every item you bring into your home, one must go. This applies to household items, clothing, magazines, everything.

Rule #2: Periodically purge your belongings. (This part is easy if you follow Rule #1.) Once a year is good. Twice a year is better. Make it part of your spring cleaning ritual, preferably before cleaning so you have less to clean!

Rule #3: Take care of the small things and the big things will take care of themselves. By paying closer attention to the little things, you can gain more control over clutter — and over your life.

Once you get rid of clutter, how can you keep it from coming back? Following are more than 85 sure-fire ways to keep clutter out of your life forever.

Paper Clutter

Cancel unread or unwanted subscriptions. You may be entitled to a refund of your unused subscription.

Don't sign up for a subscription because of a sweepstakes. Ordering does not increase your chances of winning. By law, all entries received must be included in the sweepstakes and you are not required to purchase anything.

Put a self-imposed limit on the number of subscriptions you receive, which might be half the number you receive now. If you miss any of them, you can always buy an issue from time to time or resubscribe at a later date.

If you haven't read one issue of a magazine before the next one arrives, throw away or recycle the older magazine. If this happens twice in a row, cancel your subscription.

If you don't read the daily newspaper on the day it was published, it's old news. Recycle it and start fresh with today's paper.

Recycling one copy of a medium-size daily newspaper every day of the year saves five trees. If you don't have pick-up service, take them to the nearest recycling center.

File daily to avoid buildup of paper clutter.

When you file something in a folder, see if there's something in the folder that can be thrown out.

Don't automatically accept fliers that are handed to you on the street. If you do, toss them in the first wastebasket you see.

Think twice before picking up free brochures and pamphlets. Read them on the spot, if you can, and then put them back. Take home only those to which you will respond immediately. Better yet, jot the contact information in your daily planner or notebook.

If you find yourself thinking, "I might be able to use this someday," ask yourself if it's really worth saving. Even if you do need it later, most things are not that difficult to get again.

Once a year, purge folders and papers from your filing cabinet.

Gift Getting

Cleaning expert Don Aslett says, "Treat unwanted gifts like flowers. Yes, they express a sentiment you appreciate. No, that doesn't mean you have to keep them forever."

Never accept something from someone unless you can start using it immediately. It's tempting when someone says, "Would you like this? I never use it and it matches your (blank)." Don't be fooled; you'll never use it either. Someone else's junk can quickly become yours.

Learn to say "no thanks" to things you don't want or need. Do not physically touch the item; it will be that much harder to say no.

As far as gifts go, only keep what you want. It may sound harsh, but the harsh reality is that unwanted or unused items clutter your home and you hate clutter!

If someone asks what you want for your birthday or other holiday, either make a specific request or insist they don't get you anything. Tell them you're trying to unclutter your life. Otherwise, you're likely to end up with something you really don't want or need.

If someone does give you a gift you don't want or need, thank him or her with all your heart and then pass the gift along to someone who could really use it. That way, at least two parties benefit from the gift giving. You still retain "the thought that counts" and someone gets an unexpected surprise. By sharing the gift, you are sharing the joy of gift giving.

Talk with your family about gift giving at major holidays. Many families put the names of family members in a hat and draw one name to buy for. It's easier on everyone and makes it more likely that you will receive something you really want or need. Ask yourselves if you need to give gifts at all.

Kick the Shopping Habit

Consider buying less in general. Do you really need so much stuff?

Think of the amount of time you spend shopping and use that time to do something nice for yourself or someone else. You'll feel good and you'll save money!

Go shopping only when you need something. Go with a list and stick to it.

To minimize impulse buying, leave your credit card at home. If you're willing to pay cash for an item, it's generally something that you really love or need.

Before buying an article of clothing, ask yourself: Will I wear it this week? If not, don't buy it. (Exception: shopping for an upcoming special occasion with a set date and time.)

When you buy a new piece of clothing, get rid of one piece. It keeps your wardrobe weeded of stuff you never wear.

If you see something you want, walk away from it. Go to a different store, get a drink, or use the restroom. If you really want or need that item, it will be worth the walk back.

Don't go to garage sales unless you're looking for something in particular. If you do buy something, know in advance what item at home you're going to eliminate and eliminate it when you get there.

Don't buy in bulk unless you have a place to store these items. Leaving them out just creates clutter. (Do buy in bulk anything that you use regularly to save yourself last-minute trips to the store.)

Before you buy any organizing product, ask yourself if you could just eliminate or minimize the things you were planning to organize.

Don't buy just because something is on sale. Buy because you either need it or love it.

Buy clothes in coordinating shades. You'll need fewer shoes and accessories to go with your outfits if you stick to the basics. You can plan your wardrobe around two or three basic colors for each season. Not only does it make daily dressing easier, but packing for a trip is simpler because you aren't tempted to add things that don't mix or match.

Stop buying videotapes. Borrow them from the library or from friends (and return them) or tape from television.

Determine how many outfits you really need for each season, based on your lifestyle, social commitments, and job. You may find that 10 outfits are plenty.

Instead of spending lots of money on all-new styles every season, develop a wardrobe of classic styles. You can always update your wardrobe each season with a few less-expensive tops, shoes, and accessories. But remember the cardinal rule of maintaining a clutter-free home: for every item you add, one must go!

Purchase new items only to replace items that are worn-out.

Choose either gold or silver jewelry. Think about your preference. Which do you wear most often? Chances are, that's the one that looks best on you. In general, silver tones look better on fair-skinned people and gold tones look better on darker-skinned people or people with olive complexions.

Think twice before buying souvenirs. Take photographs or keep a journal instead.

Remember that the very best things in life are free. Instead of spending money on stuff you won't use or need a year from now, spend time with a friend or family member or with a good book.

~

Don't buy something if you already have something that can do the same job.

Daily Rituals

Every time you turn on a faucet, let it be a reminder to cleanse yourself of clutter.

~

Get in the habit of doing one thing at a time. When you try to do more than one thing at once, you run the risk of doing neither well. And often it can make more work.

~

Get in the habit of finishing what you start.

~

If you catch yourself thinking, "I can do this later," stop and do it now.

~

Do as much as you can, whenever you can.

~

Treat yourself to a small reward for each task you complete.

Take 15 minutes before you go to bed and straighten up the house every night.

Don't keep what you don't want. Do keep things you love or use.

Set a limit on saving shopping bags, plastic containers, and boxes. Pick a number and stick to it.

Think twice before automatically keeping an item. Do you need it? If yes, for what? Will you need it this year? If not, find a place to store it for easy retrieval at a later date.

When deciding what to save and what to toss, err on the side of ruthlessness.

If you make a mess, clean it up right away.

Use five minutes whenever possible to reduce clutter. (Five minutes is better than zero minutes.)

Take the extra 30 seconds or five steps it takes to put something away. It's more work and takes much longer to come back to it later.

Always keep your keys and pocketbook, wallet, or briefcase in the same place.

〜

Spend time alone every day to unclutter your mind and spirit.

〜

If you're always too tired at night to pick up, try getting up 15 minutes earlier each day and start your day with a ritual of uncluttering. Unclutter while your coffee is brewing or tea is steeping. You may find you come to enjoy the extra 15 minutes each morning. That's an extra one hour and 45 minutes each week.

〜

Clean one drawer each evening.

〜

Get yourself in the frame of mind that you can't save everything. If you're not going to use it, get rid of it.

〜

Remember the one lesson you learned in shop or home economics class? Clean up while you work.

〜

If getting dressed in the morning creates a mess, figure out what you're going to wear in the evening when you have more time to hang clothes up and put clothes away.

If you come across something you haven't used in a while, put it in storage. The next time you come across it, you will know that if you haven't used it, you don't need it. Get rid of it. This works very well for clothes.

Hang up your coat when you walk in the door. If you put it on the back of a chair or throw it down, you just have to pick it up later.

If it's hard for you to throw out junk, think about that before you bring anything into the house.

Impose your will over clutter. Remember that IT is not in control of you. You are in control of IT.

Rejoice in the simplicity of an uncluttered home!

Keep at it.

Submit to the present evil, lest a greater one befall you.

— Phaedrus, a.d. 8

Periodic Purges

Clean the garage once a month.

Clean off your desk once a month. Only put back what truly belongs on your desk and find a place for everything else.

Plan a party or invite guests frequently. Getting ready for the party is fun and gives you extra incentive to unclutter.

In January each year, clean out your files and make room for the new year's files.

Make a list of projects you want to tackle and how much time you think each one might take. When you have some time, pick one from the list.

Set aside a specific time each week for uncluttering. If it takes more than an hour, let that be your early warning system that you need to focus more on daily uncluttering.

Get rid of whatever you haven't used in a year. Throw it out or box it up. If you haven't needed anything in the box within six months, throw out the whole box.

Resell or donate used items as often as possible.

Once a year or so, rearrange your knickknacks and framed photographs and eliminate any that are no longer meaningful.

When you start a new project, create a file folder for it and keep all related documents in the folder.

If you can afford it, hire a housekeeper to come in at least once a month, which will allow you time for uncluttering projects.

Have a garage sale periodically. Make it a special family event and go out for pizza afterward.

When you have a garage sale, have your kids go through their stuff, too, and let them keep the money.

Final Thoughts

Celebrate official unclutter holidays:

March 24	National Organize Your Home Office Day
August 3–9	Simplify Your Life Week
September 3	Do It! Day
October 5–11	Get Organized Week

Keep your recycling bin near the garbage can. If you have to carry bottles and cans more than a few feet, it's more likely you'll leave them near the sink or on top of whatever horizontal surface is convenient.

Always deal with the small stuff. Left to itself, the small stuff can add up quickly to a big mess.

Set the table with flowers and candles before leaving for work. Or just cover the table with a nice tablecloth.

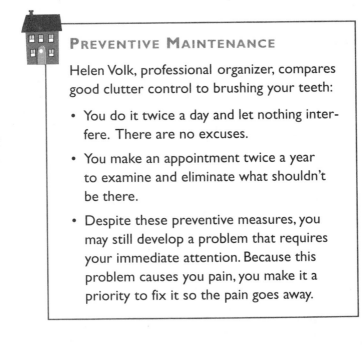

PREVENTIVE MAINTENANCE

Helen Volk, professional organizer, compares good clutter control to brushing your teeth:

- You do it twice a day and let nothing interfere. There are no excuses.

- You make an appointment twice a year to examine and eliminate what shouldn't be there.

- Despite these preventive measures, you may still develop a problem that requires your immediate attention. Because this problem causes you pain, you make it a priority to fix it so the pain goes away.

Learn to ask for help when you need it.

In your spare time, look around to rethink why you have stuff certain ways. Do I need it? Why do I have it? Is it best there? Will I use it? Then cut it down. Or throw it out.

Strive for excellence, not for perfection. There's a thing called the diminishing law of returns for which perfectionism rarely pays out.

Congratulate yourself!

Resources

National Association of Professional Organizers (NAPO)
1033 La Posada Dr., Suite 220
Austin, TX 78752-3880
(512) 206-0151
www.napo.net

Information about professional organizers or a referral to professional organizers in your area.

Messies Anonymous
5025 SW 114th Avenue
Miami, FL 33165
(800) MESS-AWAY
www.messies.com

Support group information or free introductory newsletter. (Please send SASE for newsletter.)

National Study Group on Chronic Disorganization
1142 Chatsworth Drive
Avondale Estates, GA 30002
(404) 231-6172

Reading list of books for the chronically disorganized.

Let's Get It Together
P.O. Box 590860
Houston, TX 77259
(281) 286-9512
freeweb.pdq.net/bman

On-line organizing consultation (first session free).

For advice from professional organizers on getting and staying organized, visit Discussion Forum at organizerswebring.com. You can also search the Webring by state to find a professional organizer near you.

To join on-line classes in getting organized, visit GET-O-LIFE's Web site at getolife.hypermart.net.

To sign up for a free E-mail discussion list on household organization, send an E-mail to listserve@maelstrom.stjohns.edu with the following command in the first line of your message:

> SUBSCRIBE Decluttr
> firstname lastname

Substitute your name for the words "firstname lastname." Please note that "Decluttr" is spelled without the second "e."

Organizing Products

For storage solutions, contact the following companies to request a catalog, shop on-line, or for more information about retail stores and distributors in your area.

The Container Store (Elfa®)
2000 Valwood Parkway
Dallas, TX 75234
(800) 733-3532
www.containerstore.
  com

Crate & Barrel
311 Gilman Avenue
Wheeling, IL 60090
(800) 451-8217

Get Organized!
600 Cedar Hollow Road
Paoli, PA 19301
(800) 803-9400
www.getorginc.com

Hold Everything
P.O. Box 7807
San Francisco, CA
  94120-7807
(800) 421-2264

**Kraftmaid Kitchen
  Cabinetry**
15535 South State Avenue
Middlefield, OH 44062
(800) 654-3008
www.kraftmaid.com

Lillian Vernon
100 Lillian Vernon Drive
Virginia Beach, VA 23479
(800) 285-5555
www.lillianvernon.com

Office Max Online
8100 Tyler Blvd.
Mentor, OH 44060
(800) 788-8080
www.officemax.com

Reliable Home Office
P.O. Box 1502
Ottawa, IL 61350
(800) 735-4000
www.reliable.com

Rubbermaid
1147 Akron Road
Wooster, OH 44691
(330) 264-6464
www.rubbermaid.com

Simple-Living Resources

The Dollar Stretcher
P.O. Box 23785
Fort Lauderdale, FL 33307
(954) 772-1696
www.stretcher.com

Visit The Dollar Stretcher Web site for current and past issues of this weekly newsletter dedicated to "Living Better . . . For Less." Search for and read articles and tips on a wide variety of topics including home organization, space management, and time management. Or send $2 (U.S.) to the address above for a sample issue.

GET-O-LIFE
1225 Vermont
Quincy, IL 62301
(217) 228-0434
getolife.hypermart.net

GET-O-LIFE *is a monthly newsletter and excellent resource for information, ideas, and motivation to help you work smarter, not harder. For a sample copy, send $1 to the address above. Visit the Web site to sign up for an on-line class in organizing or to post a question on the Home Organization Bulletin Board.*

The Simple Living Network
P.O. Box 233
Trout Lake, WA 98650
(800) 318-5725
www.simpleliving.net

The Simple Living Network is an on-line service with thousands of pages of information, tools, and resources for people who want to live a simpler, healthier, more environmentally conscious lifestyle. The Web site features a free weekly periodical.

The Center for a New American Dream
6930 Carroll Avenue,
  Suite 900
Takoma Park, MD 20912
(301) 891-ENUF
www.newdream.org

The Center for a New American Dream is a private, nonprofit organization dedicated to shifting and reducing consumption while fostering opportunities for people to lead more secure and fulfilling lives. Contact the Center for a free sample issue of the quarterly newsletter Enough!

Index

Other Storey Titles
You Will Enjoy

Keeping Life Simple, by Karen Levine. The book offers seven guiding principles to help the reader assess what's really satisfying and then offers hundreds of pertinent ideas about how to create a lifestyle that is more rewarding and less complicated. Paperback. 160 pages. ISBN 0-88266-943-5.

Keeping Work Simple, by Don Aslett and Carol Cartaino. Well-known time management expert and crusader against clutter Don Aslett offers practical tips for simplifying any work environment to achieve maximum performance. Paperback. 160 pages. ISBN 0-88266-996-6.

Tips for Your Home Office, by Meredith Gould. Lively, first-hand advice for creating the most comfortable, professional, and productive home-office environment possible. Gould offers ideas for managing time, work flow, and much more. Paperback. 160 pages. ISBN 1-58017-003-X.

Too Busy to Clean?, by Patti Barrett. This witty, realistic handbook is filled with shortcuts and tricks for getting organized, cleaning just about anything, and making cleaning more tolerable and efficient. Paperback. 160 pages. ISBN 1-58017-029-3.

Feng Shui Tips for a Better Life, by David Kennedy. With this easy-to-use, easy-to-understand resource, even beginners can use the ancient Chinese art of Feng Shui to attract desired life changes in the areas of health, romance, career opportunities, and more. Paperback. 160 pages. ISBN 1-58017-038-2.

These books and other Storey books are available at your bookstore and home and garden center. Order directly from Storey Books by writing to 210 MASS MoCA Way, North Adams, MA 01247, calling 1-800-441-5700, or visiting www.storey.com.